HIGH
EXPECTATIONS

HIGH
EXPECTATIONS

The Remarkable Secret
for Keeping People
in Your Church

THOM RAINER

BROADMAN
& HOLMAN
PUBLISHERS

Nashville, Tennessee

Published by Broadman & Holman Publishers, Nashville, Tennessee
Page Design and Typesetting: TF Designs, Mt. Juliet, Tennessee

Dewey Decimal Classification: 254
Subject Heading: CHURCH LEADERSHIP/CHURCH GROWTH
Library of Congress Card Catalog Number: 98-27122

Scripture quotations are from the NEW AMERICAN STANDARD BIBLE. ©
Copyright The Lockman Foundation, 1960, 1962, 1968, 1971, 1973, 1975,
1977, 1995. Used by permission.

Library of Congress Cataloging-in-Publication Data

Rainer, Thom S.
    High Expectations: the remarkable secret for keeping people in your
church / by Thom S. Rainer.
        p. cm.
    Includes bibliographical references and index.
    ISBN 0-8054-1266-2 (pbk.)
    1. Church attendance. 2. Church management. 3. Church growth.
I. Title.
BV652.5.R351999
254'.5--dc21

                                                    98-27122
                                                    CIP

1 2 3 4 5 03 02 01 00 99

To
R. Albert Mohler, Jr.
President of the Southern Baptist Theological Seminary
with gratitude for his heart for evangelism and missions
and vision to create
The Billy Graham School of Missions, Evangelism and Church Growth

and always to
Jo
a gift from God
of encouragement, joy, and love

Contents

List of Exhibits

Acknowledgments

My name appears on the cover as the author of this book. For the uninitiated, that means that the words you read are my own. I wrote the manuscript that became a book.

This book, however, is far from a solo effort. Indeed, it would not be a reality without the concerted efforts of a great team.

Sherrie Drake typed the entire manuscript. She made numerous corrections (of my mistakes!). She met tension-filled deadlines with grace and dignity. And she put up with my overdrive personality that wants everything done yesterday, even when I fail to get things done until tomorrow. This book indeed is as much Sherrie's as it is mine.

Debbie Ethridge is our graphic artist in residence. The plethora of charts, graphs, and illustrations are all her handiwork. Debbie somehow was able to have a baby in the midst of her work.

Grady Sutton, my research assistant, did an unbelievable amount of research work for this project. Grady has an uncanny sense for detail as well as great organizational skills. When I ask him to "just do it," I know the work will be extraordinary.

Chuck Lawless is one of the "rising stars" in the world of evangelism and church growth. Chuck devised the survey that was the foundation for this research. He also gathered the data and began the initial interpretation. This book has Chuck's "fingerprints" all over it.

Numerous other professors and doctoral students should also be credited for this work. This team from Southern Seminary is an extraordinary group. Thank you, guys. You make me proud to be at Southern, and you make work a joy.

My wonderful family has once again shown their love and patience in enduring yet another book. God has blessed me with the greatest sons on earth. Thank you Sam, Art, and Jess. What did I ever do to deserve such precious gifts as you three boys?

Then the heart of the Rainer family, my wife Jo, has demonstrated again her grace and love to me. When I grow weary with the research, travels, and writing, I find the greatest happiness in knowing I can come home to a wife of such beauty and joy. Thank you, Jo. I will never say it enough: "I love you."

One final word. This project was delayed because of the sudden and unexpected death of my mother, Nan Rainer. God blessed me with a mom of incomparable love for the first forty-two years of my life. I guess it is expected that grown children grieve publicly only a short while when their parents die. So I have maintained a front of composure, but deep inside I have shed a million tears.

I know you are in heaven, Mom. I could not be more certain of your salvation in Christ. But my theology is such that I am unsure if you can read these words or see the depth of my grief. Perchance you are able to know what I have written, please hear the words of a son who hurts deeply.

One day I will see you again. In the scope of eternity, the time will be short. But from my earthly perspective, the days are longer and sadder than I ever imagined. Thanks, Mom, for a life of love. I will see you soon.

Thom Rainer
Louisville, Kentucky
Easter Sunday, 1998
(The promise of the resurrection)

Churches That Reach Them
and Keep Them

"If I could name the most pressing issue in our church," the pastor told me, "it would be the issue of losing members through inactivity or transferrng to another church." An associate pastor in the Midwest had a similar concern: "We have added 411 members in four years. That's a pretty impressive number." But his joy was obviously tempered by another issue. "But even with over 400 additions, our attendance has only increased by 75 in those four years. Something's wrong!"

"You would think that my ministry would be the ideal situation. I have been at the church for eleven years. The people love me. And I can't complain about my salary." The pastor's demeanor told me that something in his church was certainly less than ideal. He continued: "You know, even though we are one of the leading churches in the state in baptisms, the real story isn't being told. We are losing people almost as fast as we gain them. Our back door is wide open!"

The Problem of the Open Back Door

For as long as I have been in ministry, I have heard church leaders talk about "back door" problems. While the "front door" refers to new members or gains in attendance, the "back door" typically means loss of members or decreases in attendance. I have spoken with leaders of numerous denominations and independent churches, and the problem seems to be alarmingly common in American churches. People are leaving our churches by the thousands each day, and others are quietly becoming less and less active.

Two years ago I led a research team to study churches that were reaching people for Christ. The results, reported in my book *Effective Evangelistic Churches,*[1] demonstrated that these churches were focusing on several basic issues in order to evangelize lost persons. The study also indicated that some of the more common approaches used to reach people for Christ were largely ineffective.

The breadth of that first study may have set it apart from other research on evangelistic churches. In the midst of that comprehensive project, our research team quickly saw that another project of equal detail would be needed. Though these churches were adding many members through conversion growth, many were also experiencing an exodus of members. And even if a particular church was not seeing large losses of membership, it may not have seen attendance gains that would have been proportionate to the number of people added to the church. Like the church mentioned at the beginning of this chapter, the total number of new members did not translate into similar gains in attendance.

Our research team desired to receive even more detail than we did in our first study. Under the leadership of Dr. Chuck Lawless, a research instrument was devised that included nearly thirty pages of questions and data input. Despite the incredible number of hours each church had to put into the instrument, we were delighted that nearly three hundred churches participated in this study. As a consequence, you the reader are about to discover insights from churches in what is perhaps the most comprehensive study of its kind.

A Look at Two Churches

Before we examine some of the more technical data in this study, let us look at two of the churches that provided us some of the insights for this book. Their stories give us the spirit that will be evident in so many of the churches and their leaders whom you will meet.

Friendship Baptist Church
Litchfield, Connecticut

We travel first to the northeastern United States to the small town of Litchfield, Connecticut. Darril Deaton has been the pastor of Friendship Baptist Church for five years. The church has experienced growth from under 90 in attendance to over 200 in one year's time. More importantly,

99 people have been baptized in just two years, and many more people have accepted Christ through a number of mission activities.

Friendship is a church that is not only reaching people, it is keeping them as well. Three-fourths of those added to the church in recent years are still active in the church today. This healthy assimilation rate is even more remarkable in light of the fact that 90 percent of the new Christians had no previous relationship with the church.

When Pastor Deaton was asked about the key to the closing of the back door, his response was straightforward: "The pastor is the main disciple-maker by example; I encourage every area of the church ministry, at every age level, to be disciple-making. I also lead several groups where I train others to make disciples."

This assimilation and discipling by example is key to the good results experienced by Friendship. But such an example by the pastor requires a clear communication of that vision to the membership. For Pastor Deaton, the communication comes through several means, but the primary communication vehicle is the sermon. And like nine out of ten of the pastors in this study, preaching was rated as one of the most exciting aspects of their ministries. A similar number of the pastors declared committee meetings to be the least exciting aspect of their ministry. These men had found ways to spend time in those ministries that make the most difference in the lives of people.

Friendship Baptist Church is a high-expectation church. Some of the expectations placed upon prospective members include the following:

- attendance in a new member orientation class,
- commitment to attend a discipling program,
- commitment to tithe to the church,
- regular attendance in worship services,
- regular attendance in Sunday School classes, and
- commitment to doctrinal guidelines.

The issue of expectations was heard clearly in the comments made by the pastor: "New members and new believers are discipled on their level and nurtured through the early stages of discipleship. Soon they begin choosing for themselves places of service, areas of involvement, and they become regular in worship and ministry-related activities." The new members and new believers know that their acceptance into the church is accompanied by clearly established expectations.

Another factor that enhances the successful assimilation taking place at Friendship Baptist is a vision statement that most of the church members understand and own for themselves. Whereas a mission statement sets forth the common purposes of all churches, a vision statement articulates God's specific plan for a specific church at a specific time. Listen to the specific vision for Friendship:

> We will confront every person in Northwest Connecticut with the gospel of Christ in order to expand the kingdom, and we will locate specific people and places where Christ would have us establish ministries and make disciples.

Where do most prospective and new members hear the vision and learn about expectations? In the case of Friendship Baptist, a great level of importance is given to the new member orientation class. Like so many churches in this study, this class is critical in establishing the expectations for membership. The topics covered in Friendship's new member class are comprehensive:

- doctrine of the church,
- church government and polity,
- membership requirements,
- policies for disciplining and excluding members,
- expectations of members after joining,
- witness and evangelism training,
- training in spiritual disciplines,
- church covenant,
- inventory of spiritual gifts,
- explanation of the church's mission and vision,
- church staff and leadership,
- ministry and service opportunities in the church,
- expectations of tithing and further giving,
- support of missions through the Cooperative Program,
- understanding baptism,
- understanding the Lord's Supper,
- tour of the church's facilities, and
- understanding the concept of spiritual armor.

Despite the incredible level of expectations evident at Friendship Baptist Church, Pastor Deaton is still not satisfied. He told us that "we are not as organized as we should be, and we need an up-to-date, streamlined mission statement." Such was the attitude of most of the leaders whose churches are in this study. Their churches are doing very well in retaining members, but the pastors are always looking for ways to improve.

Immanuel Baptist Church
Sallisaw, Oklahama

John Ewart has been the pastor of Immanuel Baptist for over five years. Sallisaw is a small Oklahoma town with a population of under 10,000. The members of the church are relatively young, with 70 percent of the people under age 50. In the past two years of record, the church has added 135 members, half of those by conversion growth. In that same period, the church has lost only 18 members. The church recently broke the 300 barrier in worship attendance.

Pastor Ewart describes himself as both high-task and high-relationship oriented. He emphasizes both relationships with people and "getting things done." Immanuel Baptist has been open to his leadership and to change as long as adequate study, prayer, and time have been a part of the process.

The pastor sees the Sunday School as the most critical factor in the assimilation process. He notes the inestimable value of this organization in closing the back door: "We use the small groups that the Sunday School provides to help us build relationships among the new members. Then we can get them more involved in other ministries and activities." The Sunday School was one of only three factors or ministries that Immanuel felt was essential in the closing of the back door.

Like most of the effective-assimilation churches in this study, Immanuel expects much of its new members. Some of the expectations include:
- commitment to spiritual gifts development and service in the church,
- commitment to tithe to the church,
- regular attendance in Sunday School and worship services, and
- commitment to follow specific doctrinal guidelines.

After the churches completed our survey, we asked them if they discovered any needs to improve assimilation in their churches. The leaders of Immanuel saw a significant deficiency because the church did not require that prospective members attend a new member class, nor did they have such a class at the time of the survey. Perhaps one of the most significant findings in this study was the vital importance of a new member class. That finding will be the topic of an entire chapter in this book.

The Study Conducted

After two years of studying evangelistic churches in America, our research team was excited about the opportunity to do further research on the "back door" or assimilation issue. As with any study, determining the beginning point is often one of the most challenging steps. From our experience in the previous study, we knew that churches of different denominations and backgrounds keep statistical records differently. We therefore began with Southern Baptist churches, with the plan to add non-Southern Baptist churches later. Such was the process we followed in our first study.

As I presented the research of the first study around the nation, I was often asked how the non-Southern Baptist evangelistic churches compared with the Southern Baptist churches. Interestingly, the only significant statistical variance between the two groups was in worship styles. Of the nearly 250 different variables, the two groups were amazingly similar. In other words, evangelistic churches had more in common with *one another* than they did with churches in their own denominations.

I realize that some will question our looking at only Southern Baptist churches in this first phase of the study. We are fairly confident, however, that this group of churches will be representative of churches around our nation, according to the criteria required to be a part of the study. Such was the case with our first project; such should be the case with this effort.

The next issue we addressed was which Southern Baptist churches would be eligible to be included in this study. The first response our research team made was that we should continue to look at evangelistic churches. As one member of the team commented: "We are not really interested in researching churches that are merely retaining members. We need to study those churches that are reaching them *and* keeping them."

As a consequence of this attitude, we first determined that eligible churches must be reaching at least twenty-six persons per year. In Southern Baptist churches, this number was represented by total annual baptisms. We further determined that the churches must have a baptismal ratio (resident members to total baptisms) of less than 20:1. In other words, the church reaches at least one person per year for every twenty members. Only 4 percent of Southern Baptist churches meet both criteria.

This criteria was consistent with our first study of evangelistic churches. Now with this pool of eligible churches, we sought to determine which churches were retaining those people they were reaching. We then looked at the total number of people added to the church each year and how those additions affected the Sunday School attendance the following year. For example, a church may add 32 people to its membership. If the church had perfect retention, all 32 of those people would attend Sunday School the next year, and Sunday School attendance would increase by 32. Thus, a church with an average attendance of 100 would increase to 132 the following year. We would then assign that church a retention rate of 100 percent.

The 287 churches that were eligible and participated in this study were divided into two equal groups: those with the highest retention rates and those with the lowest retention rates. The retention rates ranged from a low of negative 22 percent (the church had a decline in attendance despite a large number of additions) to a positive 112 percent (the church had attendance increases that were greater than the number of members added). This study will compare the significant differences between the higher-assimilation churches and the lower-assimilation churches.

Should Sunday School attendance be the key data in determining assimilation effectiveness? Would worship attendance be a better indicator of church health? In our previous study on evangelistic churches, we found a direct correlation between evangelistic health and the health of the Sunday School. This relationship proved true not only for the Southern Baptist churches but also for the over 500 other churches in subsequent research. The health of these small groups in churches is a clear indicator of the health of the church. And in over 95 percent of the churches in our nation, the primary small group is the Sunday School.

The Questions Asked

The appendix to this book provides the research instrument used in this study. The twenty-eight-page document required hours of preparation time for each church. We are delighted and grateful that nearly three hundred churches participated in this lengthy process. Our research team also conducted follow-up interviews, both on-site and by telephone, to nearly one-third of the participating churches. The result, we believe, may be the most comprehensive study ever on assimilation in churches.

You, the reader, should remember throughout this book that every church studied was first an evangelistic church. You therefore will be reading about churches that reach *and* keep people. And you should also remember that assimilation was not determined by the number of people who remained on church rolls. We were looking for those members who remained in active attendance in the churches.

What were some of the key areas we addressed in this project? Our lengthy survey was divided into the following ten major areas.

Basic church information. This data provided us with a wealth of statistical information. We learned of membership additions, deletions, and levels of activity and involvement. The churches also gave us key demographic and socioeconomic information as well.

Church staff information. In this section we were given vital information on the senior pastor and other church staff. We were told about key areas of leadership, including preaching styles, preferred ministry tasks, leadership styles, and influences on leadership.

The church's understanding of assimilation. The primary concern here was to discover the *what* and the *how* of the church's assimilation process. What was the perception of assimilation and its importance in the life of the church? How did the church make intentional efforts to close the back door?

The church's mission/vision/direction. We attempted to discover if a relationship existed between the clear articulation of the church's mission and vision and the effectiveness of retention. The results, discussed in chapter 9, may surprise you.

Visitors and visitation. Why did those who visited these churches first come to the churches? What did the churches do to receive them?

Church membership requirements/expectations. This chapter communicates some of the most critical and vital findings of the study. It supports the thesis of the book that churches with higher expectations are more likely to retain and assimilate members. The reader may be surprised to discover just what is expected of persons who desire to be a part of these high-expectation churches. We also examine the phenomenon of the new member class in an entirely separate chapter.

The training of disciples. The research team examined a plethora of ideas concerning the approaches to discipleship taken by the churches. Over thirty different ideas were studied, including the use of spiritual gifts inventories and assessments.

Pastoral care. How do the churches continue to care for the members *after* they join? Why do people leave these churches?

Missions. What level of mission activities take place in the church? How is a mission emphasis related to assimilation?

Other information. In this portion of the study, we were interested in hearing from these church leaders about their ideas for assimilation, particularly for those areas where we did not ask all the questions that needed to be asked. A majority of the churches surveyed provided us with the names of recent converts and members. We were thus able to ask the new members themselves what led them to the church and what keeps them at the church.

The Pathway of This Book

The volume of data we received was a bit overwhelming. I am grateful to a research team that was able to make sense and draw conclusions from all the information we received.

Because so much information was available, I have attempted to present and evaluate key issues in the next chapter. After that chapter, the book then looks at some of the more critical issues in greater detail. You the reader will have a plethora of graphs and charts to review throughout the book. These illustrations should provide you with clarity that will supplement the narrative of the book.

After completing our first major research project on evangelistic churches, I was greatly encouraged to see how God was working across our land. After completing this project on assimilation, I am even more encouraged.

Yes, I am aware of surveys and studies that indicate that the American church is in trouble. I am aware of the reports that tell us of the declining effectiveness of churches in our culture. Indeed this project does nothing to refute those reports. What this book will report, however, is that some churches in America are experiencing true growth, and that the same churches are assimilating those they have reached.

Throughout this book you will discover that these successful churches do not necessarily have the perfect formula of a great demographic location, perfect facilities, megachurch programs and ministries, and superstar leaders. Yet they reach people, and they keep those they reach.

The most encouraging aspect of this study is that *your* church can be among these successful high-expectation churches. The churches in this study have no magical formula or obscure methodologies. To the contrary, their focus is more on the basic biblical issues that are often ignored by many churches in our contemporary culture.

Thank you for joining me on this journey to over three hundred churches across our land. I think you will find the results of this study encouraging, challenging, and exciting. And I pray that you will be able to use portions of this book to make a difference in your church and in the kingdom. Now let us begin our trek into the world of high-expectation churches.

CHAPTER 1

How They Close the Back Door

> Throughout the New Testament, those who were saved became active members of an existing local church, or local churches were formed and they became active in them.
>
> Elmer L. Towns

Choose a typical Sunday morning in the United States. And on this typical Sunday, let us take a hypothetical visit to a church selected at random. The church is a Christian church; it may be independent, or it may belong to a denomination. Let us stretch our imagination a bit and make ourselves visitors from first-century Jerusalem, where the first Christian church is experiencing explosive growth.

While we are amazed at the world two thousand years later and marvel at all of the technological advances, we are visiting for another purpose. Our brief journey into twenty centuries of future is made to see how the church is doing after two millennia. We have chosen a church in a relatively new nation called the United States.

Before entering into the church building for worship services, we are told that the church has five hundred members. We are pleased that a typical American church has such a healthy numerical membership. Our pleasure, however, is quickly turned to despair when we enter the sanctuary. Our quick count of those present tells us that only slightly above two hundred members are worshiping together on this typical Sunday. Where, we exclaim, are the nearly three hundred who are absent?

We are further dismayed to discover that only 175 attended the time of Bible study that is called Sunday School. How could it be that only one-third of these Christians come together to study God's Word? We had originally expected to find all 500 members present, worshiping together, studying Scripture, and doing ministry. We become physically ill to find out that less than 70 members of this typical American church are involved in ministry. We return to first-century Jerusalem with heavy hearts and a report that the future church is very unhealthy, perhaps even dying.

Indeed, the early Christians would have trouble imagining the plight of the American church today. But it comes as no shock to us two thousand years later that less is expected of church members today than civic organizations expect of their members. We have dumbed down church membership to the point that it means almost nothing!

While I could offer some interesting possibilities to explain the pathetic condition of the church today, such an excursion would be beyond the scope of this study. Instead we will examine churches that defy contemporary trends. We will look at churches that are both reaching and keeping people. We will see churches in which a large proportion of the membership is actually involved in ministry.

The Southern Baptist churches we studied were in various parts of the country. In exhibit 1–1 below, the diversity of the churches' sizes is evident. In subsequent studies we will be examining churches from other backgrounds and even more diverse locations. Throughout this project we are attempting to discern what is different and distinct about churches that not only reach people for the Savior but also keep them in active involvement in the church.

Exhibit 1–1
Sizes of Churches

Average Attendance	Number of Churches	Percent of Total
Less Than 100	20	7.0
100–299	146	50.8
300–499	69	24.1
500–699	19	6.6
700–999	7	2.4
1,000–1,499	10	3.5
Above 1,500	16	5.6
Total	287	100.0

Eight Surprises

Our research team had certain expectations. Some of these expectations may better be called biases. But when I speak of surprises, I am speaking about results that are contrary to or rarely discussed in much of the church growth literature. In other words, some of the following results do not fall in line with the conventional wisdom in the field.

Long Pastoral Tenure Is Highly Correlated to Effective Assimilation

The average tenure of a Southern Baptist pastor is just over two years. For all churches in the United States, the tenure is only slightly better at three years. But the average tenure of pastors in the high-assimilation churches is 9.83 years. The lower-assimilation church pastors had an average tenure of four years. Why would longer-term pastorates engender more effective assimilation?

The answer to that question will be more fully developed in chapter 5, where we look at the profile of a typical pastor in a high-expectation church. For now let us see some of the dynamics of tenure as it relates to assimilation.

Donald Sharp is the pastor of Faith Tabernacle Baptist Church, an African-American congregation in Chicago. The church averages about 400 in two morning worship services. The church is retaining 90 percent of the new members that have come into the church in recent years. The church is clearly a high-expectation church for its new and longer-term members. Expectations are set regarding new member classes, tithing, attendance, participation in Sunday School, and adherence to doctrinal guidelines.

Faith Tabernacle has transitioned to higher expectations because of the congregation's trust level of its pastor. Pastor Sharp has led the church through many changes, and the church has followed its leader *who has been pastor for over thirty-three years*.

Listen to one member's comments about her pastor as he has led the church through change: "Our pastor recognizes that through all changes there must be prayer. He often emphasizes principles used by Jesus in relating to people and to the congregation. His understanding of the Word of God characterizes the policies he refers to in leading our church through change."

Though new pastors can often implement significant changes in the "honeymoon" years of their ministry, some changes take time. Rarely will a church transition from a low-expectation church to a high-expectation church in a short period. Such changes require time, and they require the leadership of a pastor who is committed to see the church through these changes. We will develop this issue more fully in a later chapter.

Location Is Not a Factor in Healthy Assimilation

Like the discovery we made in our earlier study of effective evangelistic churches, location is not correlated to assimilation. The churches that effectively closed the back door were found in open country and rural areas, in small towns and inner cities, in the suburbs, and in small- and medium-sized towns. Exhibit 1–2 shows the variety of locations of the churches in this study.

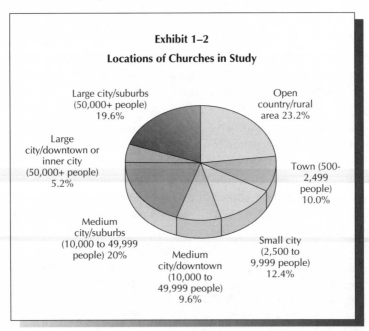

Exhibit 1–2
Locations of Churches in Study

Large city/suburbs (50,000+ people) 19.6%
Open country/rural area 23.2%
Large city/downtown or inner city (50,000+ people) 5.2%
Town (500-2,499 people) 10.0%
Medium city/suburbs (10,000 to 49,999 people) 20%
Small city (2,500 to 9,999 people) 12.4%
Medium city/downtown (10,000 to 49,999 people) 9.6%

Mission Statements Are More Important Than Vision Statements

In this study we made a distinction between a mission statement and a vision statement. We defined mission as "the primary purposes in which all Christian churches should be involved; these purposes typically include worship, evangelism, discipleship, ministry, and fellowship." We then defined the vision as something related to a specific church: "God's *specific* plan for a *specific* church at a *specific* time."

The majority of these churches felt it was critical for their members to understand the purpose of the church. The leaders were less concerned about knowing exactly what God had planned for the church at a specific time. Exhibits 1–3 and 1–4 depict clearly the emphasis of mission statements over vision statements. More than six out of ten churches responded that they had mission statements. But only four out of ten churches had vision statements.

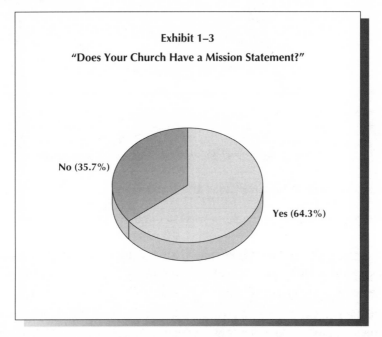

Exhibit 1–3
"Does Your Church Have a Mission Statement?"

No (35.7%)

Yes (64.3%)

A pastor in Texas commented regarding a vision statement: "We are happily ignorant not knowing that we don't have one." His humorous point was stated in a variety of ways by other church leaders. While some found the articulation of a vision statement necessary to provide direction and resource allocation, the majority felt that a specific plan was too confining. They also commented that the vision is dynamic, that God's specific plans are ever changing. The leaders expressed concern that a vision statement might be obsolete by the time it was formulated and approved by the church.

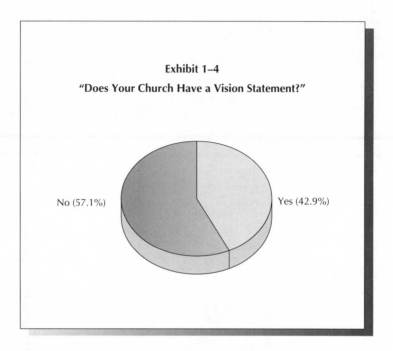

Exhibit 1–4

"Does Your Church Have a Vision Statement?"

No (57.1%)   Yes (42.9%)

Expository Preaching Can Close the Back Door

Although expository preaching was rated the highest single factor in our earlier study on evangelistic churches, we were surprised to discover that it was strongly correlated to closing the back door. Indeed in this study, expository preaching was second only to Sunday School among the methodologies that are effective in assimilation.

We defined expository preaching as "primarily explanation or commentary on the biblical text; expounds the central idea of the text; often includes preaching through a book of the Bible." Other types of preaching approaches that were stated in the study were topical preaching, thematic preaching, and narrative preaching. Exhibit 1–5 shows the dominance of expository preaching over the other preaching styles. Each pastor estimated the percentage of sermons that reflect each of the four different styles.

Though the pastors did not limit themselves to one style of preaching, on the average they preached expository messages over 60 percent of the time. How does expository preaching become a method for assimilating members? How can an expository sermon close the back door?

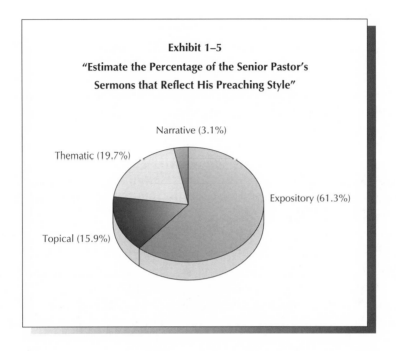

Exhibit 1–5
"Estimate the Percentage of the Senior Pastor's Sermons that Reflect His Preaching Style"

Narrative (3.1%)

Thematic (19.7%)

Expository (61.3%)

Topical (15.9%)

Over and over again these pastors explained to us that Christians who are equipped to do the work of ministry are more likely to remain active in the church than other members. One of the most powerful type of equipping approaches is the teaching of God's Word through contextual preaching. As the Bible is taught in its context week after week through expository preaching, the Holy Spirit teaches the people and convicts them about their service and places of ministry. This form of equipping is also able to reach the most people, since the worship service is typically the point of highest attendance.

We asked the respondents to rank forty different programs and ministries according to their importance in the overall assimilation process. Additionally, the churches could name other factors we did not list. The responses were to be on a scale of one to five as follows:

1. not important at all,

2. only slightly important,

3. important,

4. very important, but not essential, and

5. essential.

Sunday School was rated the highest with an amazing average response of 4.91. But preaching was not too far behind with a response score of 4.40, and the great majority of the sermons preached are expository messages.

Douglas Criswell has been the pastor of Grace Baptist Church in Dayton, Ohio, for four years. In just one year Sunday School attendance jumped from 80 to 150. The church is experiencing amazing growth, while effectively closing the back door. Pastor Criswell rated preaching a "five" (essential) in the assimilation process. He estimates that 80 percent of his sermons are expository messages.

How does he see the expository sermon to be an essential element in the assimilation process? "My sermons must lead people to growth," Pastor Criswell told us. "These messages help people find the ministry God has called them to. As a consequence, they get involved in ministry and become a vital part of the church as a whole." And that involvement means that the back door is closed. Those involved in meaningful ministry rarely leave the church.

The Pastor "Gives Away" Ministry

From a biblical perspective, one might expect a significant amount of equipping from the pastors of high-assimilation churches. Paul clearly gave this mandate to the leaders at the church at Ephesus when he said: "And He gave some as apostles, and some as prophets, and some as evangelists, and some as pastors and teachers, for the equipping of the saints for the work of service, to the building up of the body of Christ" (Eph 4:11–12). The surprise came not in that pastors were willing to give away some of the ministry that was expected of them, but in the intensity with which they delegated ministry.

Only 15 percent of the pastors believed that the pastoral care of the church members was their primary responsibility. Indeed, as we will see shortly, the Sunday School was the key assimilation arm of the church because the Sunday School members were expected to care for those in their classes. In an earlier work, I spoke of an "Acts 6 revolution" that was a major trend in the church today.[1] In this passage we find the Grecian Jews complaining against the Hebraic Jews because their widows were not receiving their daily distribution of food. The apostles, instead of trying to do more ministry themselves, sought and equipped laypersons to do this pastoral ministry.

The apostles made it clear that they would turn the ministry over to others: "And the twelve summoned the congregation of the disciples and said, 'It is not desirable for us to neglect the word of God in order to serve tables. But select from among you, brethren, seven men of good reputation, full of the Spirit and of wisdom, whom we may put in charge of this task. But we will devote ourselves to prayer, and to the ministry of the word'" (Acts 6:2–4).

A pastor in Georgia reflected the sentiments of many of the pastors we interviewed: "I used to worry about criticism when I would turn over ministry to the members of the church. And a few did complain. But now I wouldn't have it any other way. My people are becoming more involved by doing ministry I once did, and I can devote more time to prayer and sermon preparation."

The Critical Importance of Youth and Children's Ministry

The churches that were successfully closing the back door emphasized the priority of involving and ministering to the Bridger Generation, those young people born between 1977 and 1994.[2] This generation is one of the most receptive groups to the gospel, and they respond well to high expectations. Exhibit 1–6 depicts the vital role youth and children's ministries play in assimilation. Only Sunday School, the morning worship service, and expository preaching ranked higher in importance as ministries vital in assimilation.

What is the relationship between youth and children's ministries and assimilation? In our follow-up interviews, we learned that the sheer size of the Bridger Generation necessitated focused efforts at retention. This generation, seventy-two million strong, is the second largest generation in America's history. Only the Baby Boomer Generation is larger.

Perhaps more importantly, we learned that focused efforts to assimilate these young people often resulted in entire families becoming involved in a church. A California pastor commented: "We have seen several nominally active families become very involved with our church after their kids became active. A teenager's father told me that he could not just sit on the sidelines while his daughter was demonstrating such spiritual growth. We are surprised to see more and more kids lead the way spiritually."

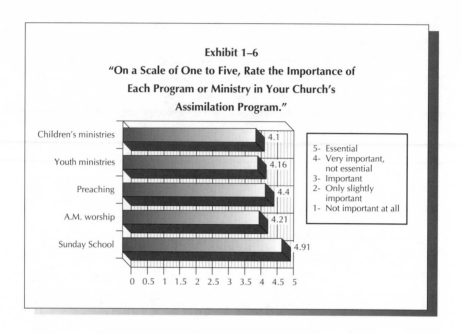

Exhibit 1–6

"On a Scale of One to Five, Rate the Importance of Each Program or Ministry in Your Church's Assimilation Program."

Children's ministries — 4.1
Youth ministries — 4.16
Preaching — 4.4
A.M. worship — 4.21
Sunday School — 4.91

5- Essential
4- Very important, not essential
3- Important
2- Only slightly important
1- Not important at all

0 0.5 1 1.5 2 2.5 3 3.5 4 4.5 5

The Worship Service as a Means to Assimilation

Rarely does one hear that the worship service can function in the assimilation role. We read about the service as the front door, but this study indicates that it can also close the back door. Two important elements, we were told, must be present for the worship service to be an assimilation factor.

First, expository preaching, mentioned earlier, equips Christians for ministry and service. This facet of the worship service is the teaching and equipping time for church members.

Second, the pastor and other leaders use the worship time to communicate high expectations to the congregation. One worship and music leader told us that high expectations can be communicated in parts of the service other than preaching. "Every hymn and chorus we sing should inform the believer of the demands of discipleship," he said. "Even the offertory should be handled in such a way that the members realize that giving is a natural and expected part of the Christian life."

Weekday Ministries Are Not Effective in Closing the Back Door

We were also surprised to discover that the churches in this study did not see weekday ministries as a positive factor in assimilation. We included in the weekday ministry category day care, recreational activities, weekday cell groups, church affiliated schools, and a catch-all "other weekday ministries." Exhibit 1–7 shows that the assimilation effectiveness of these ministries ranged from "not important at all" to "only slightly important."

We learned that most weekday ministries are designed to serve Christians rather than engender high expectations. "We have a day care that serves ten times more people than those who work in the day care," an associate pastor from Florida told us. "And all of those who work in the day care are paid. We believe that the ministry is important, but we don't fool ourselves into believing that people are truly being discipled by this ministry."

Again we heard a common theme. Those ministries that expect much of believers are more likely to help close the back door. Weekday ministries apparently did not fit that definition.

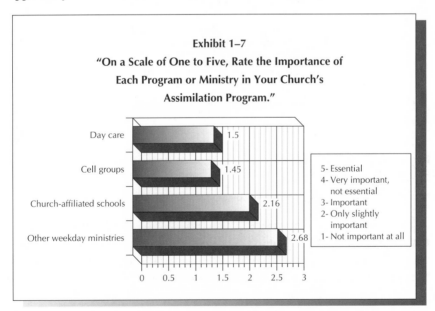

Exhibit 1–7
"On a Scale of One to Five, Rate the Importance of
Each Program or Ministry in Your Church's
Assimilation Program."

Day care — 1.5
Cell groups — 1.45
Church-affiliated schools — 2.16
Other weekday ministries — 2.68

5- Essential
4- Very important, not essential
3- Important
2- Only slightly important
1- Not important at all

Seven Major Issues

Throughout this book you will be introduced to numerous issues related to churches that are effectively closing the back door. In this chapter we will examine some of the major back-door factors in brief, with a view toward looking at them in greater detail in the remaining chapters.

Exhibit 1–8 shows some of the major assimilation methodologies of these churches. But methodologies alone cannot explain the dynamics of churches that reach people and keep them. Some of the factors are more subjective than methodological. Let us look at some key issues in both the methodological and the more subjective categories.

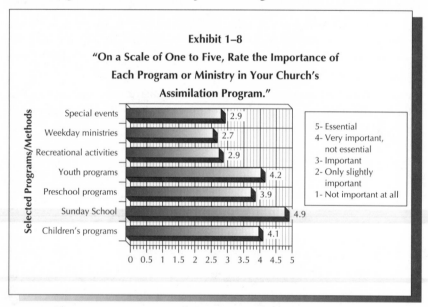

Exhibit 1–8

"On a Scale of One to Five, Rate the Importance of Each Program or Ministry in Your Church's Assimilation Program."

The High-Expectation Factor

Regardless of the methodological approaches of the effective assimilation churches, all demonstrated clearly stated expectations in all of their ministries. E. Donald Hattaway is pastor of Emmanuel Baptist Church in Blackshear, Georgia, a town of under ten thousand. Pastor Hattaway ranks Sunday School as the primary assimilation tool of the church. The Sunday School assimilation approach obviously has been successful. In one year the church added one hundred members, and most of that growth has been assimilated into the Sunday School.

If we concluded that the mere existence of a Sunday School program ensures the closing of the back door in this and other churches, we would be missing a major element in the churches' success. These churches not only have a Sunday School program in place; they *expect* their members to make the program work.

"Our church uses the Sunday School organization to contact every member each quarter," Pastor Hattaway told us. "The Sunday School teachers carry the responsibility of organizing their classes into care groups. This system ensures close contact with each member. The pastor is notified by the Sunday School if pastoral care is needed."

Hear the expectations in the words of the pastor. Each member is contacted quarterly with the expectation that they attend. The teacher is responsible not only for teaching but also for organizing the class into pastoral care units. And the care group leaders are the primary persons responsible for ministry to church members. They will contact the pastor only if the ministry need is great.

Repeatedly we heard about effective assimilation methodologies that worked only if the ministries carried with them high expectations of those involved. Such is the primary conclusion and thesis of this study. *Effective assimilation churches have one primary characteristic that sets them apart from churches that do not keep their members in active involvement. Effective assimilation churches had high expectations of all of their members.*

The Primacy of the Sunday School in Closing the Back Door

In the next chapter we will see in detail how Sunday Schools are utilized to close the back door in the high-assimilation churches. For now let it be said with clarity and emphasis that no single methodology was as effective in closing the back door. As exhibit 1–8 depicted, the importance factor of Sunday School was 4.91, which means that almost all of the high-assimilation churches view this methodology as "essential."

The issue that is obviously raised is that of the Southern Baptist bias in the study. Is Sunday School considered essential because of contextual factors related to the Southern Baptist denomination?

I might have conceded this bias had our research team in a previous study not faced this same issue. In our study of 576 effective evangelistic churches, we found the Sunday School to be one of the most important factors in the churches' success.[3] Since all of these churches were Southern

Baptist, I expected that the Sunday School factor was something unique to the denomination. Indeed, most of the critics of my first study spoke of a Southern Baptist bias. At the time I could not disagree.

But when I tested the survey against nearly five hundred non-Southern Baptist churches, I was surprised to find little to no statistical differences, except in worship styles. Though the verdict is still out, I fully expect again to see Sunday School as a critical assimilation tool in *all* churches that close the back door effectively, not just the Southern Baptist churches.

The Critical Role of Visitor Follow-up

High-expectation churches believe that assimilation actually begins well before someone decides to join a church. Indeed when someone visits their churches, leaders make certain that the visitor is "touched" in a number of ways. This follow-up may involve a personal letter from the pastor, a telephone call, or perhaps a visit to the home of the person who came to church.

What do these actions communicate? First, they tell the members of the church that they are expected to make contact with those who visit the church. It is not an optional issue. Follow-up is imperative.

Second, these actions communicate to the visitor that the people of the church are involved in ministry. In other words, the prospect sees that membership carries with it expectations.

Many of the churches in our study gave us the names, addresses, and telephone numbers of new Christians who had joined their churches in the past year. Our conversations with these believers yielded some valuable insights. Henry is a new Christian from a church in Tennessee. Although he understands clearly that salvation is by grace alone, he also understands the cost of discipleship better than many long-term Christians.

"When I accepted the Lord," Henry said, "I knew that I had not done anything to deserve being saved." He paused for a moment before continuing. "But I knew that being a Christian and belonging to this church meant that something would be expected of me. I learned that lesson when I received seven different contacts from church members when I first visited the church. I thought to myself: *These Christians take their beliefs seriously.* Their commitment inspired me to become a Christian and eventually to be involved in ministry like they are."

The "New Program": New Member Classes

New member classes or prospective member classes have become so common that they are virtually considered a regular program in these high-expectation churches. The class is the most-frequently-used point of entry where the expectations of membership are articulated. Indeed, these classes were so common in the high-assimilation churches that their absence was a rare exception.

In our follow-up interviews, we discovered even further the importance placed on new member classes. Numerous pastors and church staff told us that these classes were minimized in the past. But today in these churches the classes are critical. Corona Baptist Church in Chandler, Arizona, is typical in its approach to new member classes among the high-expectation churches. At present the class is not required for membership, but the expectations are that prospective or new members will attend.

Since this issue is one of such importance, we are going to treat it with greater depth in two ways. First, the entirety of chapter 7 will address the new member class. Second, Charles Lawless is in the process of writing an entire book on the topic, with a release date shortly after this book. The material we gathered on this critical issue is simply too massive to be contained in one chapter.

Prayer: The Forgotten Power of Assimilation

One of the greatest contrasts between the high-assimilation churches and the low-assimilation churches was the role of prayer in closing the back door. In the high-assimilation churches, prayer played a critical role in retention. The low-assimilation churches, however, did not rank prayer highly in the assimilation process.

The contrast can best be illustrated on the scale we introduced earlier in this chapter. As exhibit 1–9 depicts, the high-assimilation churches ranked prayer with an average of 4.77, closest to the point on the continuum called "essential." The low-assimilation churches, however, ranked prayer with an average of 2.98, "important," but not essential.

How did prayer fit into the process of assimilation? Though the approaches varied, one of the more frequent responses we received was that new Christians were taught to become involved in prayer from the beginning of their new birth. They were instructed, particularly in new member classes, to become involved in corporate prayer, and they were

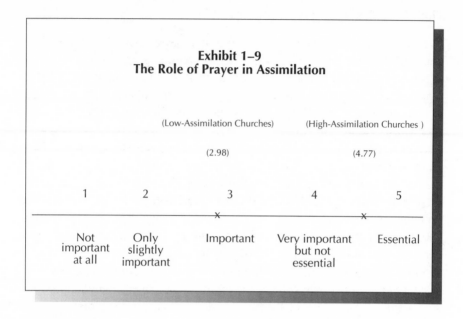

**Exhibit 1–9
The Role of Prayer in Assimilation**

(Low-Assimilation Churches)   (High-Assimilation Churches)

(2.98)   (4.77)

1	2	3	4	5
Not important at all	Only slightly important	Important	Very important but not essential	Essential

discipled to become men and women of personal prayer. Apparently, the new member or new Christian who is taught to pray is much more likely to remain active in the church.

Leadership, Leadership, and Leadership

The role of the church leader, with a particular emphasis on the pastor, is critical in the assimilation process. While not all pastors of the high-assimilation churches had identical leadership traits, they did have some common characteristics. For example, the most significant leadership "teacher" was their own successes and failures in ministry. These men were not afraid to attempt major tasks for God. Even if the attempt was a failure in the world's eyes, the pastors viewed the experience as positive because of what they learned from it.

Indeed, they ranked their experiences as major influences over such other possibilities as seminary training, mentors, conferences, books, or leadership experts. The implications of this influence are profound. We will examine more fully such implications and numerous other leadership factors in chapter 4.

Doctrine: Clarified and Followed

The high-expectation churches were unapologetically conservative in their doctrine. In our follow-up interviews with various church leaders, we were told about their high view of Scripture. Indeed a full 100 percent of the pastors interviewed used the word *inerrancy* to describe their understanding of the trustworthiness of the Bible.

But the church leaders were not content merely to affirm certain doctrines and beliefs; they were determined that the church members understand biblical truths. For the longer-term members, the teaching of doctrine came primarily through expository preaching and strong Sunday Schools. For the new Christians who joined the church, the new member class served as the first point of introduction to basic biblical truths.

Closing the Back Door: The Expectation Factor

Get ready to discover the details of how churches reach people *and* retain them in active membership. You will meet leaders from nearly three hundred churches who will take you beyond theory to that which is really taking place in effective churches. Some of your ideas may be affirmed by this study. But, if you are like me, some of your presuppositions may be challenged.

Throughout this book you will see the word *expectation* or the phrase *high expectation*. These words in varying ways describe the primary finding of the study. Churches that expect more from their members are more likely to retain them in active membership. This discovery is good news. God's church is being taken more seriously by many churches. Membership means more than a walk down an aisle and a hearty "amen."

Indeed, the high-expectation church of today seems to have some of the characteristics of the first-century church. Membership means ministry. Salvation by grace results in works. And inactive membership is fast becoming a contradiction in terms. We thus take our first step into the inner workings of these churches by asking what methodology is primary. The answer is Sunday School. Perhaps that answer is no surprise. In the next chapter, however, you may find some insights into Sunday School that are surprising. Welcome again to the world of high-expectation churches.

CHAPTER 2

Above All: Sunday School and the Back Door

Many church leaders have helped perpetuate the myth for twenty or so years. The myth is that Sunday School is no longer effective evangelistically or as an assimilation tool. And those who believed the myth are suffering the consequences today.

Don Cox

After nearly a decade of researching two thousand churches of different sizes, locations, and denominations, I cannot say that I am surprised that Sunday School was rated so highly as an assimilation tool. My surprise in this study, however, was the *intensity* by which the church leaders expressed their beliefs that Sunday School is *the* chief assimilation approach.

Essentially the churches told us that involvement in Sunday School was the gauge by which they determined if effective assimilation had taken place. Burkemont Baptist Church in Morganton, North Carolina, averaged 566 in Sunday School in the latest data we received. Amazingly, that level of attendance was 93 percent of the average worship attendance of 610. And in the previous year Sunday School attendance was actually higher than worship attendance.

Burkemont is typical of the churches we studied. The leaders believe that involvement in Sunday School is tantamount to effective assimilation. For example, one of our survey questions asked the following: "Please list the guidelines you use to determine if a church member has been successfully assimilated into your church, that is, how do you know when a member has 'a sense of belonging and is thus involved in the ministry of the church'?"

Burkemont's response was straightforward and typical: "We follow up with new members to get them involved in Sunday School classes." But the church goes well beyond expecting that new members merely attend Sunday School. The church also utilizes Sunday School outreach directors and "class caregivers" to get each new member involved in *ministry*.

Santuck Baptist Church is located in Wetumpka, Alabama, near the capital city of Montgomery. The church experienced a significant increase in Sunday School attendance, from 187 to 264 in just one year. The pastor, Morgan Bailey, rated Sunday School a "5" (essential) in its importance in assimilation.

Interestingly, Santuck has a four-step strategy to assimilate new members, none of which explicitly mention Sunday School. The strategy includes:

1. Believing—leading people to a life-changing commitment to Christ.

2. Belonging—guiding people to commit to Christ's church through believer's baptism and meaningful church membership.

3. Becoming—helping people become what God has created them to be, particularly through involvement in discipleship.

4. Behaving—encouraging people toward regular attendance, ministry involvement, community impact, and personal evangelism.

Indeed, the "Santuck strategy" includes goals beyond Sunday School involvement, such as spiritual gift assessment, ministry involvement, and completion of a new member class. But no member is considered "assimilated" until he or she is actively involved in Sunday School.

The church recognizes the critical importance of Sunday School. An annual Sunday School worker appreciation banquet recognizes those who work in this critical ministry. New workers are also installed annually, recognizing the importance of their positions and ministry.

I could repeat over two hundred church responses to the importance of Sunday School for assimilation, but the material would be redundant. The data is convincing and overwhelming: Sunday School is critical. At this point we are more interested in telling the "why" and "how" perspective of Sunday School. But first, please allow me a few words about my own pilgrimage.

Confessions of a Sunday School Skeptic

In the 1980s I had become a "Sunday School skeptic." Though I did not try to dismantle the Sunday Schools in the churches I pastored, I certainly was not a leader in making the organization stronger and more evangelistic. If anything, the Sunday Schools of my churches suffered from pastoral neglect.

I was not alone in my sentiments. Many of my peers were like me, enamored with some of the latest methodologies and innovations to help a church grow. Sunday School just seemed a bit old-fashioned compared to the "cutting-edge" information we were receiving from a plethora of sources. Indeed, I had my doubts that Sunday School would be a viable growth and assimilation tool in the twenty-first century. But two developments led me to see my biases in a different light.

First, I noticed that many of the highly touted growth innovations had an unusually short life span. What was hyped to be *the* methodology for the church was gone in a year or so. In other words, it proved to be little more than a fad. In the meantime, Sunday School continued to be the dominant program in most churches.

Second, I embarked on my first major research project on the local church in the early 1990s. I was serving as a pastor, but my church allowed me the time to visit other churches and interview their leaders.

Over the course of two years, I had made contact with nearly two hundred different churches. About one hundred and fifty of the churches were from my denomination, and the remaining fifty were from six other denominations. What I discovered both disturbed me and convicted me.[1]

In almost every church, I heard pastors and leaders talk about the role of Sunday School for their evangelistic growth and assimilation. Though many did share some new and innovative methodologies, almost all the leaders said that their sustained growth would have been impossible without the Sunday School.

Any lingering doubts I had about Sunday School were erased when my research team and I at Southern Seminary conducted a study of 576 churches in America.[2] I learned once again that the leading churches in our nation value the Sunday School in growing a church and assimilating members.

One would think that I would have no surprise when the strength of Sunday School became evident in yet another research project. This time, however, the overwhelmingly positive response regarding the Sunday

School surprised me. No assimilation methodology came close to Sunday School in effectiveness. The leaders told us the methodology was number one, with no real competition.

What inherent characteristics of Sunday School make it the chief assimilation tool in evangelistic churches today? How has the methodology of antiquity weathered the storms of change to remain effective? What did we learn from nearly three hundred evangelistic churches? To these questions we now turn.

Sunday School and the Back Door

Exhibit 2–1 compares the Sunday School's assimilation effectiveness to other approaches. As a reminder, the values in parentheses can be understood by the following scale:

1	2	3	4	5
Not important at all	Only slightly important	Important	Very important but not essential	Essential

No methodology was deemed more effective than the Sunday School in retaining members. And, as we shall see later, the leaders in these churches understand well the value of Sunday School, and it has thus become a high priority in their own ministries.

For example, Ken Stalls, pastor of South End Baptist Church in Frederick, Maryland, not only ranked Sunday School with a "5" in assimilation effectiveness; he placed a comment by his evaluation stating that "it was the key element."

Another one of the many pastors who recognized the critical importance of Sunday School was Kenny Qualls, pastor of Springhill Baptist Church in Springfield, Missouri. For Springhill, the measurement of successful assimilation begins with "involvement in (not merely enrollment in) Sunday School."

Though the ways churches utilize the Sunday School in the assimilation process are numerous, the success of retention can be categorized into six major factors. Look at these fascinating issues addressed by the leaders.

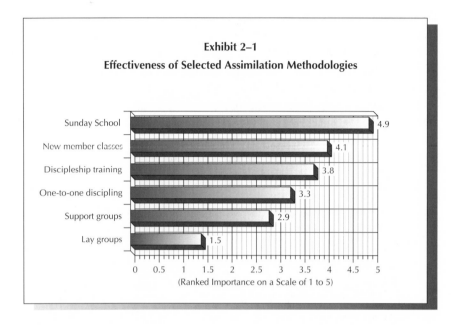

Exhibit 2–1

Effectiveness of Selected Assimilation Methodologies

Sunday School — 4.9
New member classes — 4.1
Discipleship training — 3.8
One-to-one discipling — 3.3
Support groups — 2.9
Lay groups — 1.5

0   0.5   1   1.5   2   2.5   3   3.5   4   4.5   5

(Ranked Importance on a Scale of 1 to 5)

The Expectation Factor

Sunday School is neither neglected nor accidental in the churches that are closing the back door. To the contrary, the churches that we surveyed were highly intentional in their approach to Sunday School.

Perhaps the key Sunday School issue separating higher-assimilation churches from lower-assimilation churches was that of expectations. Our research team is presently studying non-Southern Baptist churches to compare with the data we presently have on the Southern Baptist churches. I recently interviewed the pastor of a non-Southern Baptist church in the Washington, D.C. area. His testimony on the rediscovery of Sunday School is not atypical of other comments we heard.

"A few years ago," he told us, "I was ambivalent about Sunday School. I did not plan to eliminate it from our church, but I certainly was not giving it a priority." But, in 1994, he began to read and hear about churches that were rediscovering the strength of the Sunday School.

"I guess you might say I had a wake-up call," he told us. "I realized that our church had been evangelistically apathetic and that our back door was wide open. I began rethinking my lack of priority about Sunday School.

Then things began to change as our church made some intentional efforts to revitalize this ministry."

Among the intentional efforts, the most dramatic were related to raising the commitment level of those who led and worked in Sunday School. Look at some of these changes:

- Teachers would covenant to prepare their lessons each week and to attend a Wednesday-night workers' meeting where the lesson would be discussed.
- Each adult class would establish a goal to start one new class each year.
- Each class would form care groups of no more than five per group. The care group leader would have responsibility to see that ministry to the others in the group was carried out.
- Each class would have an outreach leader to make certain that all guests were contacted and members were accountable for developing relationships with unbelievers.
- Teachers and other leaders would covenant that they would arrive early for Sunday School each week.
- An annual covenant renewal service began in 1995, where Sunday School leaders made these and other commitments formally.

This church began seeing amazing results as expectations were raised. "Once we declared that Sunday School was important and that we had expectations of the leaders, the changes were dramatic," the pastor said. Attendance not only increased among the regular attenders, nominally active members began to attend regularly as well. Turnover among teachers dropped dramatically. Ministry through the Sunday School increased almost exponentially. And, for the first time in the pastor's tenure, people were won to Christ through the Sunday School organization.

Repeatedly in our research, we heard about the renewal of the Sunday School. And we heard about results similar to that of the Washington church. But, more than any other factor, we heard about the back door closing because of higher expectations.

It would appear that the Sunday School organization in many churches is suffering from benign neglect. The reasons for this neglect are numerous, but the pastors' comments could be summarized in a few categories.

Some pastors have had the same attitude I once had, that Sunday School is a tool of antiquity. They have become convinced, even though the data shows the contrary, that newer models of ministry are better. Thus, their time and energy are diverted away from Sunday School to other more "contemporary" approaches.

Others pastors have simply taken Sunday School for granted. It is the largest organization in their churches, and it will always be there, they reason. It has a momentum of its own and needs no further emphasis or attention from the pastor.

A third group told us that they had given so much attention to the corporate worship service that the Sunday School was relegated to secondary importance. Undoubtedly, the renewed interest in worship has been a blessing to churches and to their growth potential. But when Sunday School is neglected as a consequence, the wide-open front door is often countered by a wide-open back door.

In our interviews with the leaders of the higher-assimilation churches, we asked if their moving of Sunday Schools to become high-expectation organizations had caused any problems. Their answers were an unequivocal "yes." Some teachers and leaders refused to agree to stricter requirements and dropped out of ministry and service. Others resisted, implying that high-expectations in the Sunday School hinted of legalism.

Never did we hear that the expectation issue was addressed with ease. But in virtually every case, the pastor or staff member told us that the pain was worth the gains realized. A pastor in South Carolina commented, "Our desire to have greater commitments to Sunday School came at a cost. We lost some members and made others mad."

"But was the move ultimately beneficial?" we asked. "Without a doubt," he replied. "The people in our church realize more than ever that Sunday School is our primary teaching and assimilating arm of the church. And I predict it will soon become our chief evangelism arm."

The Organization Factor

I was recently leading a seminar in Wichita, Kansas, called Closing the Back Door. I spoke for approximately one hour on the importance of a quality Sunday School organization for effective assimilation. In this context I mentioned the need for care groups within the Sunday School, regular workers' meetings, ministry involvement of class members, quality teaching, enrollment emphases, and opportunities for fellowship.

At the conclusion of that particular portion of my seminar, I asked for comments and questions. One sixtyish gentleman asked how my Sunday School emphases were different from those with which he was familiar in the 1950s. His point was well made. In essence the principles have changed little, nor should they change.

What then are some of these principles? A well-organized Sunday School will integrate the principles of effective teaching, effective evangelism, the ministry of all believers, and Christian fellowship and relationships. The key words, however, in the preceding sentence were *well-organized*.

When we divided our study churches into two groups, we found some interesting relationships concerning organizational emphases. Lower-assimilation churches mentioned organizational emphases in only 32 percent of the surveys. Higher-assimilation churches cited the need for strong organization in 92 percent of the responses.

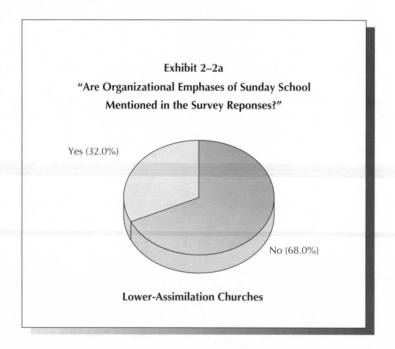

Exhibit 2–2a
"Are Organizational Emphases of Sunday School Mentioned in the Survey Reponses?"

Yes (32.0%)

No (68.0%)

Lower-Assimilation Churches

The inescapable conclusion could be paraphrased by the cliché: "Sunday School will work only if you work Sunday School." In the higher-assimilation churches, basic organizational principles were at work continuously. Teachers were trained and taught weekly. New members were assigned to Sunday School classes. Care groups were created in all classes so that ministry could be effective. Outreach and evangelism were organized through the Sunday School.

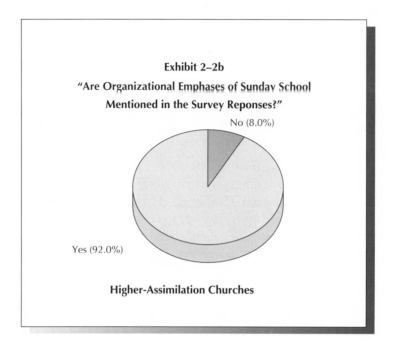

Exhibit 2–2b

"Are Organizational Emphases of Sunday School Mentioned in the Survey Reponses?"

No (8.0%)

Yes (92.0%)

Higher-Assimilation Churches

The higher-assimilation churches had strong Sunday School organizations. And that organizational quality did not occur by accident. The quality was the result of hard work, persistence, perseverance, and a willingness to suffer short-term losses for long-term gains.

Bob Lilly has been pastor of Catonsville Baptist Church for a decade. The church is located on the edge of the Baltimore city limits. The racial makeup of the church is 80 percent Caucasian, 15 percent African-American, and 5 percent Asian. Though not a large church, the Sunday School attendance jumped nearly 40 percent in one year. Also, 95 people accepted Christ and were baptized in two years.

Catonsville is experiencing significant growth for a church that had been averaging only one hundred in Sunday School in previous years. We asked Pastor Lilly how the chirch is retaining these members. He admitted that a formal assimilation process "is really nonexistent. I have been doing most of it. We have many new babies [in Christ] but who are strong [spiritually] and are often doing double duty."

What then has been the glue of assimilation in this fast-growing church? Among other methodologies, Sunday School was rated a "5" (essential). Indeed, attendance in Sunday School is one of the church's four benchmarks of assimilation.

Catonsville's story is typical in the churches we studied. The churches are growing evangelistically, but the leadership is concerned about closing the back door of the new growth. Yet when they evaluate their assimilation approaches, they discover that Sunday School has been their "glue," even when they are less than pleased about the overall success at closing the back door.

Indeed, one of the gratifying results of this study was the new awareness of Sunday School as an assimilation tool expressed by church leaders. Listen to the words of a pastor in California: "I have taken Sunday School for granted most of my ministry. This study has shown me that I must lead my church to make our organization more effective than ever. I will no longer neglect the Sunday School organization."

The Ministry Factor

Thomas James, pastor of Alpha Baptist Church in Morristown, Tennessee, has seen remarkable growth at the church. In one year alone, Sunday School attendance increased from 251 to 320. In that same year 164 people joined the church, 95 by profession of faith and baptism. Like most of the church leaders who participated in this study, Pastor James saw Sunday School as the key methodology to close the back door.

A question on our survey that produced some of the most interesting responses was: "Please list the guidelines you use to determine if a church member has been successfully assimilated into your church, that is, how do you know when a member has 'a sense of belonging and is thus involved in the ministry of the church'?"

Alpha Baptist's criteria are three. First, the member must be active in Sunday School. Second, he or she must be a regular participant in worship. And third, he or she must be involved in ministry.

Nearly two hundred of the survey churches indicated that their primary means for members to be involved in ministry is through the Sunday School. Thus, attendance in Sunday School is not the sole indicator of assimilation. Ministry through the Sunday School is a critical factor.

How do these churches involve their members in ministry through the Sunday School? The beauty of this organization is that so many possibilities are available. Below are just some of the ministries indicated by our survey churches.

1. Teaching—The most commonly associated Sunday School ministry, but certainly not the only one.

2. Care group ministry—Many churches divided each Sunday School class into care groups of four to seven persons. While a care group leader would coordinate the ministry to each member, all Sunday School class members were to be ministers within their groups.

3. Evangelism and outreach ministry—These churches indicated that about 5 to 25 percent of their members are gifted or desirous of being involved in evangelism and outreach. The Sunday School is an organization that can provide this opportunity.

4. Hospitality ministry—Most church members perceive that they have the gifts of service or encouragement. The Sunday School, through its fellowship and contact systems, uses these gifts.

5. Leadership and organizational ministry—Many Christians are particularly inclined to ministries that require keen skills or gifts in administration or organization. Certainly the Sunday School is in need of such skilled persons.

6. Prayer ministry—Over a third of the churches studied had prayer ministries through Sunday School classes. As many as half of their class members were typically involved in these ministries.

What we learned from these churches is that no organization in America today provides more opportunities for ministry than the Sunday School. The small-group movement is certainly to be lauded for its contributions to the kingdom. But, as George Barna recently noted, the movement has been on a numerical decline for the past few years. Barna cited a tendency toward weak teaching, lack of leadership and accountability, confusion of purpose, and inadequate child care as possible explanations for the downturn.[3]

For reasons we will see at the end of this chapter, Sunday School has been able to avoid these pitfalls and open the door for the ministry involvement of millions. And involvement in ministry means that a significant step has been made to close the back door in our churches.

The Relationship Factor

My mother died suddenly and unexpectedly on December 9, 1997. At the time of her death, I was in regular contact with two groups of people. The first group included my coworkers, friends, and students from Southern Seminary. Numerous people from the seminary showed an outpouring of love and sympathy toward me.

The second group consisted of people from Carlisle Avenue Baptist Church in Louisville, where I served as interim pastor for a year. I was overwhelmed to the point of tears when a group from Carlisle drove 550 miles one way to attend Mom's funeral in Union Springs, Alabama.

Other than these two groups, I had no regular contact or relationships with any particular group. I was therefore surprised and touched when I received food, visits, cards, and words of concern from another group, my Sunday School class at Springdale Church in Louisville.

For nearly three years my attendance at Springdale has been sporadic because of my outside speaking engagements and interim pastorates. But when my family and I moved to Louisville nearly five years ago, I joined Springdale and the Agape Sunday School class. I was active in the class for almost a year, and I developed strong relationships with many of the people there.

Those relationships were strong enough to engender an outpouring of love, even though my absences had been long-term and conspicuous. Indeed that Sunday School class remains my tie to the church.

Exhibit 2–3 provides a breakdown of participants in the morning worship services in the churches studied. Some of the categories are overlapping, so they do not add to 100 percent.

When we asked which of these groups were most effectively assimilated into the church, the responses were overwhelmingly clear. The two groups represented in exhibit 2–3 that are regular Sunday School attenders were least likely to leave the church or to become inactive.

A pastor in California expressed this position cogently: "Our church has tried everything to create relationships among the members: small groups, dinner clubs, family ministries, you name it. But we keep coming back to the Sunday School. That's where people get to know one another best.

We've finally gotten smart enough to decide to put our best efforts in relationship building there."

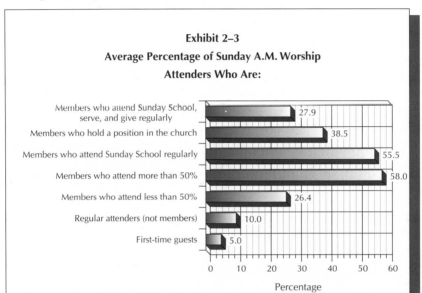

Exhibit 2–3

Average Percentage of Sunday A.M. Worship Attenders Who Are:

Members who attend Sunday School, serve, and give regularly	27.9
Members who hold a position in the church	38.5
Members who attend Sunday School regularly	55.5
Members who attend more than 50%	58.0
Members who attend less than 50%	26.4
Regular attenders (not members)	10.0
First-time guests	5.0

Percentage

The Doctrine Factor

A few studies have established the relationship between doctrinal understanding and assimilation. For example, a study of the churches in the Presbyterian Church (USA) denomination found that younger generations tend to leave the church within about twenty years if the church has a low view of biblical authority and if the doctrine of the church is not communicated clearly.[4]

Two questions may surface immediately. How is doctrine related to the closing of the back door? Why has the relationship between doctrine and assimilation been mentioned so infrequently?

The issue of doctrine and the closing of the back door is closely related to expectations and assimilation. The clear teachings of biblical truth are demanding and convicting. The Holy Spirit speaks through God's Word in such a way that the cost of discipleship is understood. No higher expectations could be placed upon believers than these truths of Scripture. And, as we have seen throughout this study, high expectations are clearly related to assimilation.

Virtually all of the higher-assimilation churches in our study used a comprehensive plan to teach the Bible to all age groups. For most of these churches, the denominational Sunday School curriculum served this purpose well.

A pastor in Colorado expressed the sentiments of many of the leaders in the higher-assimilation churches: "Needs-based studies and special emphases in Sunday School are okay for a short while. But those types of studies need to be the exception instead of the rule. Many people in the churches are woefully ignorant of the Bible. And doctrinally weak Sunday Schools are partially to blame."

The second question asked why the relationship between doctrine and assimilation was mentioned so infrequently. The primary reason is that the assimilation problem is more *long-term* than immediate. Sometimes the adverse effects of weak doctrinal teaching do not begin to show for five, ten, or even fifteen years (when an entire younger generation leaves the church). But the average tenure of pastors is far less than five years. Thus, a potential problem ten years away is not perceived to be the problem of the present ministry.

The Evangelism Factor

One of the reasons I visited the nondenominational church in the Orlando area was its remarkable evangelistic record. The church had grown from less than one hundred in attendance to nearly three hundred in just two years. And most of the growth had come from conversion of adults.

The first question I had to ask the pastor was: "How is your church reaching so many people for Christ?" I had examined the demographic data of the church's community, and the growth potential in the area was modest at best. How had the church baptized nearly two hundred people in two years?

The pastor could best be described as easygoing. His mannerisms and words reflected someone who was definitely not in a rush. His answer to my question was straightforward: "Sunday School," he said.

"Wait a minute," I responded. "You simply do not hear of churches today using Sunday School as their primary evangelistic arm."

"We do," the pastor deadpanned.

Though I had originally planned to stay at the church through Friday, I made the decision to stay for the Sunday services, particularly for Sunday

School. One class in which I had particular interest was an adult Sunday School class that had reached fourteen people in the past year. Perhaps the fact that the church kept accurate records of the number of persons baptized by Sunday School class should have been a clue to me. I was already seeing an accountability for evangelism within the Sunday School.

I arrived at the evangelistic Sunday School at 9:00 A.M., since the scheduled beginning was 9:15 A.M. Much to my surprise, not only was the teacher present, but nearly half who would attend that Sunday were already there. No one arrived later than 9:15.

The class was a bit large; approximately twenty were in attendance. But I learned that the class had started with an average of twelve at the beginning of the year and that two new classes had been started from the class in the past eighteen months. I was impressed!

Equally impressive was the fact that two-thirds of the Sunday School class members had been trained in personal evangelism in the context of their own class. On the day I attended, prayer concerns began with prayers for lost persons to whom they were witnessing. Most of these persons were coworkers or neighbors.

I would discover at the end of the class that two non-Christians were present the day I attended. When I asked the teacher how those nonbelievers felt with so much evangelistic emphasis, the response was: "Why don't you ask them?" Indeed, the teacher called the two to join our after-class conversation.

Somewhat hesitatingly, I asked the two non-Christians if they felt uncomfortable in the class today. Their response was so quick that it caught me off guard. One quickly said, "Not at all! We know these people care for us because they show their concern every day. The reason we attend is because of the love they have shown toward us."

This nondenominational church taught me some things that would later be reinforced in this study of Southern Baptist churches. Let me highlight the lessons I learned.

Lesson #1: The only reason churches are not evangelistic through the Sunday School is that they make no intentional efforts to do so. Somewhere in the recent past, many of us stopped talking about evangelism in the Sunday School, and many churches stopped doing Sunday School evangelism. We then decided that this methodology could no longer be evangelistic. Such is a myth that has no factual basis.

In our previous study on evangelistic churches, we discovered that Sunday School-based evangelism was the third most effective approach.[5] The only evangelistically dead Sunday Schools are those that have chosen this path.

Lesson #2: The Sunday School organization engenders evangelistic accountability. The time of prayer in the Orlando-area church was also a time of accountability. The members of the class came to expect relationship evangelism as a way of life because of their accountability to one another each Sunday.

Lesson #3: The Sunday School can be a natural training ground for personal evangelism. The class members already know one another. Many have close relationships. Evangelism training is often easier in such a setting.

Lesson #4: If the leaders emphasize evangelism through the Sunday School, others will follow. A pastor in Texas emphasizes evangelistic outreach through the Sunday School on a regular basis. The result? Since he began this emphasis three years ago, baptisms have tripled.

Lesson #5: Evangelism through the Sunday School will not be effective unless evangelism is a priority in the entire church. The power of the priority of evangelism was evident in this study and in our previous study.

Lesson #6: These evangelistic Sunday School classes could be called high-expectation Sunday Schools. Repeatedly in this study we heard about the biblical expectations placed on these class members. Not only do they respond with more evangelistic enthusiasm, they are also likely to remain productive and active in the church. Sunday School class members in the higher-assimilation churches describe themselves as "content," "hardworking," "enthusiastic," and "fruitful," to name a few. They had no intentions of dropping out.

Lesson #7: Sunday School-based evangelism results in more effective assimilation. I returned to the Orlando-area church one year later. The two non-Christians were non-Christians no longer. They had accepted Christ about ten months earlier. Their growth in Christ was obvious. And, like most of the new Christians in this church, they obviously intended to stay active in the church.

Perhaps the most significant lesson is that effective assimilation for new Christians is directly related to the way the people were evangelized. We reviewed the records of hundreds of church members who had made professions of faith five years earlier. We then asked the staff if these persons were primarily worship-service-only attenders or if they also attended Sunday School regularly. The contrast between the two groups was stark and amazing.

As exhibit 2–4 depicts, the new Christians who immediately became active in the Sunday School were *five times* more likely to remain in the church five years later (we did not include those who moved to another community or those who died in the "dropout" category). And those churches that were emphasizing evangelism through the Sunday School were most naturally seeing new Christians become involved immediately in the Sunday School.

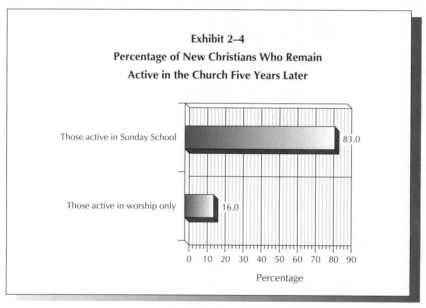

Exhibit 2–4

Percentage of New Christians Who Remain

Active in the Church Five Years Later

Why Not Cell Groups?

Look at the contrast between the assimilation effectiveness of cell groups versus Sunday School. Exhibit 2–5 shows the Sunday School ranking to be 4.91, while the cell groups ranking was 1.45. What could explain the discrepancy between the two approaches?

We asked church leaders that had utilized both Sunday School and cell groups why they ranked Sunday School higher. Four responses were given with frequency.

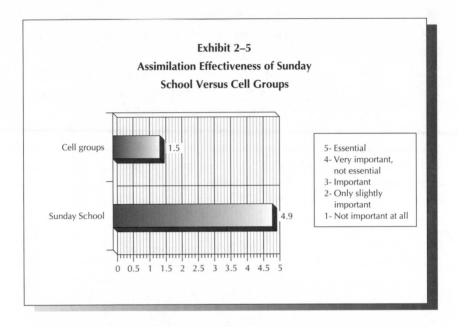

Exhibit 2–5
Assimilation Effectiveness of Sunday
School Versus Cell Groups

Cell groups — 1.5

Sunday School — 4.9

0 0.5 1 1.5 2 2.5 3 3.5 4 4.5 5

5- Essential
4- Very important,
   not essential
3- Important
2- Only slightly
   important
1- Not important at all

First, the church leaders told us that Sunday School was simply easier to organize and administer than cell groups. Typically, the cell groups met in diverse locations at many different days and times. The strength of the diverse schedule, we were told, was offset by the difficulty of maintaining basic records for accountability.

Second, Sunday School more easily included all age groups. One of the persistent problems we heard with cell groups was the issue of child care. A minister of education in Oklahoma noted: "We started cell groups in the summer with a pretty good track record. But once school started, many couples with children stopped coming. They had activities for their kids at school, or they just couldn't find adequate child care."

Third, many of the leaders in our study were concerned about the doctrinal integrity of their cell groups. Whereas most Sunday Schools used a standardized curriculum, the cell groups tended to allow the group leader to determine the study each week. Robert Wuthnow of Princeton University noted this problem in his research that found cell groups "do little to increase the biblical knowledge of their members."[6] Instead of a strong objective study of Scripture, Wuthnow noted, the cell groups "encourage faith to be subjective and pragmatic."[7]

Finally, the church leaders told us that sequencing Sunday School and worship services on the same day provided many practical benefits. "I came to realize that our cell groups were separating families for yet another day in the week," a Michigan pastor told us. "We solved many problems when we started emphasizing Sunday School as our small group. Now families can come to church together and leave together."

We must not conclude from this study that cell groups have little value. There have been too many lives changed positively to reject categorically the benefits of these small groups. Nor must we assume that Sunday School must fit one pattern (that is, Sunday morning only). But from the data we have gathered over the past four years, the traditional Sunday School has been the dominant methodology to close the back door, and it has been one of the leading evangelistic approaches.

And though this study focuses upon Southern Baptist churches, both our past and future research included hundreds of non-Southern Baptist churches. The data seems to indicate that the Sunday School model is the dominant approach for effective assimilation in these churches as well.

Above All

The research is clear if not overwhelming. Sunday School is *the* most effective assimilation methodology in evangelistic churches today. It is a place where teaching, discipleship, ministry, fellowship, and evangelism can all take place. It is the place where relationships are formed and people become connected to the church.

But the mere existence of a Sunday School does not produce assimilation. The classes must have the best and most thoroughly trained teachers. Expectations must be clear that ministry and evangelism should take place within each class. And the organization itself should be well run with good records and strong administrative leaders. Sunday School works. But only if we work Sunday School.

We have known that Sunday School is a vital component of the past for American churches. Its history is almost as old as our nation itself. But more and more the research indicated that Sunday School is not only our past, it is our future as well. And we who are leaders in the church will ignore this reality to our churches' peril.

CHAPTER 3

What Must I Do to Join This Church?

The New Testament church clearly had believers who were
committed to ministry through their local fellowship. The Scriptures never hint that their "membership" was taken lightly.

Tim Beougher

Confronted with the awesome power of God, the Philippian jailer cried
out to the apostle Paul and to Silas: "Sirs, what must I do to be saved?"
(Acts 16:30). After studying nearly two thousand churches in America for
the past six years, I heard prospective members and new converts ask this
question with a slight change of words: "What must I do to join this
church?" Unfortunately, the leaders of the vast majority of churches
responded with a nod to walk an aisle or to fill out a membership card.
Nothing else was expected or required.

Is it any wonder that the membership standards of civic organizations
are usually much higher than those of local churches? Is it any wonder that
only four out of ten Southern Baptists attend church services on any given
Sunday? Is it any wonder that church leaders are frustrated because they
cannot get their fellow church members to commit to tasks of sacrifice and
longevity?

The typical church in America today has "dumbed down" the meaning
of membership to a point where membership means nothing. The phrase
"inactive members" is often used as if it were taken from the pages of
Scripture. But in reality the only inactive members we see in the history of
the New Testament fellowship are Ananias and Sapphira as they are carried out feet first from the Jerusalem church (see Acts 5:1–11).

What has happened in the American church today where membership
or belonging to a local fellowship means so little? The early church gladly

met daily. They won the favor of those observing them. They were a magnetic fellowship that attracted thousands.

But for many church members today, Easter-only attendance is not unusual. Instead of being a magnetic fellowship attracting many, numerous churches have poor reputations in their communities. Though some differences between the first-century church and the church of today are cultural, most are theological. Our understanding of the church, discipleship, and commitment is flawed. The biblical pattern for church involvement and commitment is significantly different than the pattern in most churches today.

From the First Century to the Twenty-First Century

In this study we interviewed a pastor in the Southwest who asked to remain anonymous. "Joe" had been pastor of his church for nine years, and his frustration was high. "Our church was like a revolving door," he told us. "We would add as many as sixty members a year, but our average attendance changed only by four to six annually. People were leaving or becoming inactive as fast as new members joined."

Joe decided to do something about the situation. He realized that people who were coming to his church had no expectations when they joined. "Membership was nothing more than walking the aisle, shaking my hand, and filling out a membership card," he observed. "I shouldn't have been surprised with our wide-open back door. You get what you expect, and we expected nothing."

The pastor realized that he had the trust of most of the membership. After nine years, the members had developed a great deal of love and respect for him. "I knew I had to cash in a lot of chips to make this work," Joe commented. "But I could not let the church continue with business as usual."

Joe met with different leaders in the church. He explained to them that the low level of membership expectations had created a low-commitment church. And he suggested ways that the standards might be raised. Among those suggestions he included:

- a required membership class *prior* to joining the church;
- expectations articulated for financial stewardship and faithful attendance in worship services and Sunday School; and
- placement in some level of ministry *prior* to membership.

Over a period of eighteen months, all three suggestions became a part of the church's official requirements for membership. Even with the high trust level the pastor had earned, the transition was costly. The critics spoke of "legalism" and "autocracy." Seven entire families left the church. And even many of the supporters had their questions and doubts.

As of this writing, the pastor has been with the church fourteen years. Most of the conflict is behind, although scars remain. "I knew this change would be costly," Joe told us. "But if I had known how painful it would have been for my family and me, I probably would not have done it."

The first two years after the membership requirements changed, the number of new church members fell to half the level of previous years. But, much to Joe's joy, attendance began to increase even with the lower level of annual additions. Last year eighty-two members joined Joe's church. Only four of those members are not active in the church presently: three moved out of town and one died.

High-Expectation Membership

Alpha Baptist Church in Morristown, Tennessee, had experienced some amazing growth. In one year the attendance jumped from 312 to 577, an increase of 265. In that same year 173 joined the church, 95 by conversion. Alpha's attendance increase exceeded the number of additions significantly.

How does Pastor Thomas James explain not only the phenomenal growth but also the amazing retention? He explained to us that successful assimilation of each member is monitored closely, and a series of questions are asked. Listen to his questions:

- "Are they 'plugged into' Sunday School, where they receive contact, fellowship, friendship, and intimacy?"
- "Do they regularly participate in worship?"
- "Are they involved in other ministries and activities at Alpha?"

Clearly, Alpha Baptist Church has high expectations of its members. Indeed, the word *expectations* was heard by our research team throughout this study. A key factor in the evangelistic and retention successes of these churches was their insistence that membership must be meaningful and committed.

Signs of Expectations

In this chapter we will examine ten types of expectations of churches. All of the churches have met our criteria to be considered evangelistic churches. We will focus specifically on those evangelistic churches that are retaining their new members as well.

Keep in mind that, in our survey, we used two key words: *required* and *expected*. Most of the churches spoke of expectations more than requirements. The leaders of these churches desired to see their fellowships become a place where certain requirements must be fulfilled before membership is granted. But, more often than not, they settle for high expectations over requirements as a first step.

Relationship with Christ

We would presume that every Christian church would require all of their members to be Christians. Much to our surprise, however, only 56 percent of nonevangelistic churches we studied required an articulated personal commitment to Christ for membership. Among the evangelistic churches, 99.3 percent required a statement of a personal faith in Christ for membership.

The almost unbelievable story is that half of churches in America today do not require that their members be Christians. Some may have a level of expectation, but they are not actually asking new members anything about their personal relationship with Christ. And a significant minority of churches we studied do not even *expect* that their members will be Christians!

One very important lesson that we learned from the evangelistic churches is that they are asking eternal questions of prospective members, even if they come with membership from a dynamic church in the next state. "We don't presume anything about new members," a California pastor told us. "Every person who desires to join our church is asked pointed questions about their salvation experience. And we have led twenty-two people to Christ in three years just by asking."

The message is unmistakably clear. Every church should take seriously the evangelistic mandate when someone seeks membership. One of the reasons retention rates are so low in many churches is that, by default, an unregenerate membership has been accepted as normative.

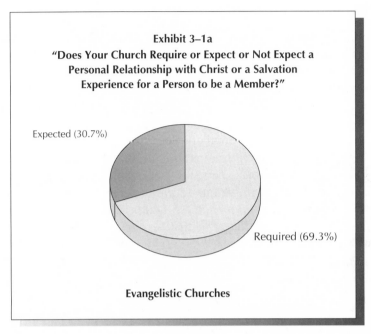

Exhibit 3–1a
"Does Your Church Require or Expect or Not Expect a
Personal Relationship with Christ or a Salvation
Experience for a Person to be a Member?"

Expected (30.7%)

Required (69.3%)

Evangelistic Churches

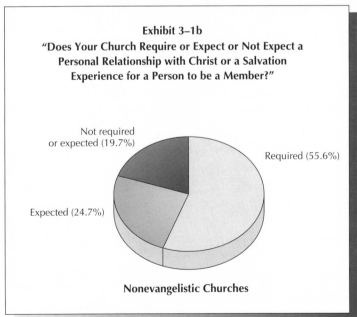

Exhibit 3–1b
"Does Your Church Require or Expect or Not Expect a
Personal Relationship with Christ or a Salvation
Experience for a Person to be a Member?"

Not required
or expected (19.7%)

Required (55.6%)

Expected (24.7%)

Nonevangelistic Churches

Baptism

Baptism is the first step of obedience for a new Christian. It is a theological mandate rather than an option to initiation. Since this first phase of our study included only Southern Baptist churches, we fully expected all of the evangelistic churches to require baptism for membership. Nearly 99 percent did so. Three churches (surprisingly) expected but did not require baptism.

The way the evangelistic Southern Baptist churches accepted baptisms was interesting. Nearly three-fourths (73.9%) accepted baptism by immersion following a salvation experience, but not necessarily baptism in a Baptist church. The remaining one-fourth required that the baptism take place in a Baptist church or, for some, a Southern Baptist church.

Again, we were surprised to find that, among the nonevangelistic Baptist churches, nearly four out of ten of the churches did not *require* baptism for membership. Exhibit 3–2 depicts the difference between the two groups of churches.

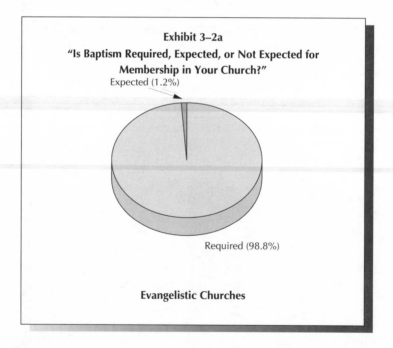

Exhibit 3–2a

"Is Baptism Required, Expected, or Not Expected for Membership in Your Church?"

Expected (1.2%)

Required (98.8%)

Evangelistic Churches

Again the contrast is stark between the two groups of churches. The evangelistic churches typically *require* baptism prior to membership. More is expected. More is required. Such will be the theme throughout this study.

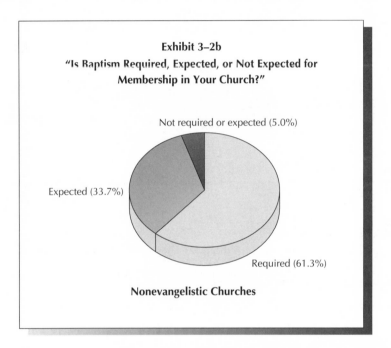

Exhibit 3–2b
"Is Baptism Required, Expected, or Not Expected for Membership in Your Church?"

Not required or expected (5.0%)

Expected (33.7%)

Required (61.3%)

Nonevangelistic Churches

Worship Attendance

Rimrock Baptist Church of Billings, Montana, has experienced remarkable growth in worship attendance. In a two-year period the attendance in morning worship soared from 290 to 410. For Pastor John Hunn, expectations are high that new members will be actively involved in worship services. He described assimilation when a member is "active in outreach in his or her job, community, and home, as well as faithfulness in worship."

Very few of the evangelistic churches in our study actually required attendance in worship as a requisite for membership. The expectation factor, however, was ever present. In various venues and through different means, the message was clear. At the very least, the church leaders told us, a member is expected to attend worship services.

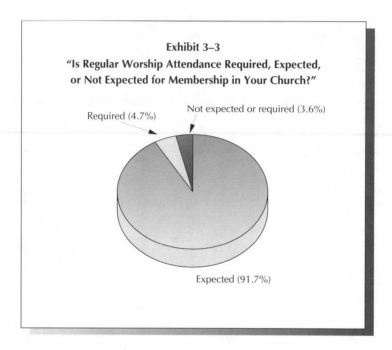

Exhibit 3–3
"Is Regular Worship Attendance Required, Expected,
or Not Expected for Membership in Your Church?"

Required (4.7%)

Not expected or required (3.6%)

Expected (91.7%)

Sunday School Attendance

In light of the previous chapter's rather detailed discussion of Sunday School, the reader might not expect that much more could be said about the topic. But one further comment should be made.

Sunday School *is* the most effective assimilation arm of the churches studied. The church leaders, however, do not merely organize a great Sunday School and hope that their members will be involved. To the contrary, every new member is expected to be a part of a Sunday School class.

In many of the churches, church membership is granted only when the prospective member is willing to join a Sunday School class. "By telling new members up front that they must be in a Sunday School class, we are sending a clear message," a New York pastor told us. "We cannot force them to attend the class, but we can expect them to do so."

A small but significant minority (41 churches) of the churches in the study granted membership only after the person had enrolled in and attended a Sunday School class. The new member, therefore, had already had some level of involvement in Sunday School prior to his or her membership in the church.

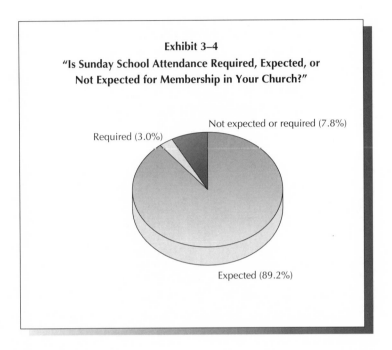

Exhibit 3–4
"Is Sunday School Attendance Required, Expected, or Not Expected for Membership in Your Church?"

Not expected or required (7.8%)

Required (3.0%)

Expected (89.2%)

Adherence to Doctrine

Doctrine matters. What churches believe and how they communicate their beliefs do matter. Higher-assimilation churches were much more likely to ask prospective members to agree to a basic doctrinal statement of the church. How did this adherence to doctrine positively impact assimilation? Listen to the comments from various leaders of higher-assimilation churches:

- "We require that all prospective members agree to our statement of faith. We may have a few each year who disagree, but it saves us from a lot of problems later on."
- "Why would someone join any organization where the beliefs are not known? People are willing to stay with our church because they have no doubt where we stand."
- "When we started articulating our beliefs to new members, our retention rate improved dramatically."
- "We actually require our new members to sign a doctrinal statement before they join the church. We have been criticized for being too legalistic, but the benefits have far outweighed the criticisms."

- "*Doctrine* has become a ridiculed word by some church leaders. Why do they have a problem being perfectly clear about what they believe?"

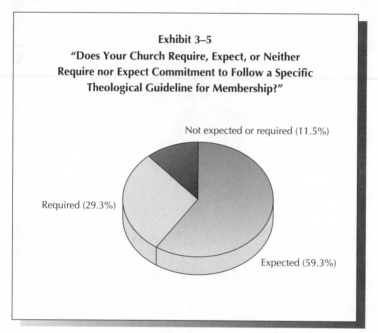

Exhibit 3–5
"Does Your Church Require, Expect, or Neither Require nor Expect Commitment to Follow a Specific Theological Guideline for Membership?"

Not expected or required (11.5%)

Required (29.3%)

Expected (59.3%)

Nearly three out of ten of the churches in our study actually *required* adherence to a doctrinal position for membership. Though many factors were expected of church members, it was unusual to see this position required by the churches.

Another six out of ten churches *expected* their members to follow an established doctrinal position. Clearly, these evangelistic churches placed a high value on their beliefs, and they believed that these biblical issues should be clear to their membership. One Tennessee pastor commented: "We are what we believe, so we had better be very clear that we expect our membership to understand and follow our beliefs."

Spiritual Gifts and Ministry

An issue that clearly set apart the evangelistic churches in our study from the general population of churches was the expectation of ministry involvement by the members. A minister of education at a large church in Alabama said: "We are gradually moving away from the position that membership in our church simply means that your name is on a member-ship roll. We have a goal that, in five more years, every member will be involved in ministry."

The churches in our study represent only a small proportion of churches in America. (Our study showed that 3.5 percent of American churches would have met our definition of "evangelistic churches.") Still, it is encouraging to see an emerging trend redefining the meaning of member-ship.

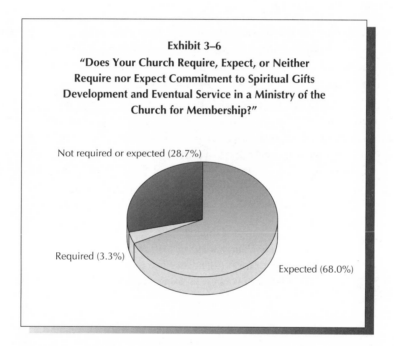

Exhibit 3–6
"Does Your Church Require, Expect, or Neither Require nor Expect Commitment to Spiritual Gifts Development and Eventual Service in a Ministry of the Church for Membership?"

Not required or expected (28.7%)

Required (3.3%)

Expected (68.0%)

Nearly seven out of ten churches in the study now expect their members to be involved in ministry as a requisite for membership. Though only a few churches actually require ministry involvement for membership, our discussions with the church leaders indicate a clear trend in this direction.

Most of the churches that expect ministry as a requisite for membership also provide spiritual gift assessment tools and inventories for their members. A pastor in Virginia addressed this issue: "While we do want them to do ministry according to their gifts and desires, we've seen too many willing but unproductive members in ministry when they are doing something that they do not like, or a ministry where they are not gifted."

I am often asked if there is a spiritual gift assessment program that is better or more popular than others. The leaders of these evangelistic churches helped us little to answer this question. No single spiritual-gifts product was chosen by more than six percent of the respondents in our study.

New Member Classes

If a single major trend could be gleaned from this study, it would be the emergence of new member classes as a common ministry in the higher-expectation churches. Indeed, this trend is so significant that all of chapter 6 will be devoted to this growing phenomenon.[1]

What is the major purpose of this class? In the evangelistic and high-retention churches, the communication of *information* is secondary to the communication of *expectations*. It is in this class where the prospective member hears what it means to be a part of the local church. He or she typically understands clearly after this class that some level of commitment is expected. Membership means much more than attendance.

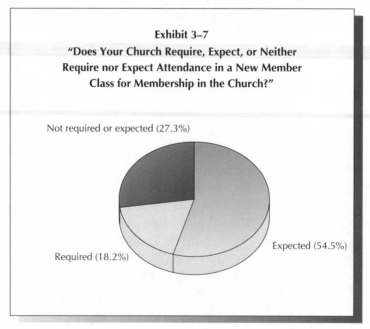

Exhibit 3–7
"Does Your Church Require, Expect, or Neither Require nor Expect Attendance in a New Member Class for Membership in the Church?"

Not required or expected (27.3%)

Expected (54.5%)

Required (18.2%)

Read with anticipation the further elaboration on this issue in chapter 6. It may be a major trend of the church in the twenty-first century.

Discipling/Counseling of New Christians

The higher-assimilation churches in this study were likely to have some formal requirements or expectations for new Christians. More than eight out of ten of the churches either required or expected each new convert to have post-conversion counseling with a trained follow-up counselor.

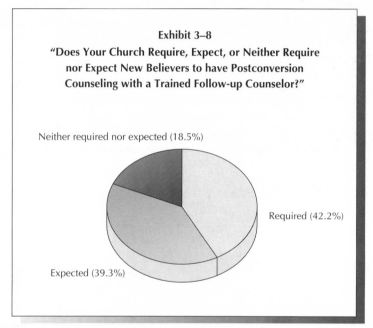

Exhibit 3–8
"Does Your Church Require, Expect, or Neither Require nor Expect New Believers to have Postconversion Counseling with a Trained Follow-up Counselor?"

Neither required nor expected (18.5%)

Required (42.2%)

Expected (39.3%)

More than 40 percent of the churches mandated a formal procedure for new believers to come into the church. The number of churches requiring this process is extraordinary. For most entry issues, expectations are more common than requirements. For new believers, however, postconversion counseling is more often required.

What is the typical process for this counseling? Usually the new believer is matched with someone of the same gender who can provide about two hours per week of instruction and mentoring. A wide variety of purchased and self-designed materials were used in this mentoring process.

Public Testimony

One of the surprises of this study was the number of high-expectation churches that *required* a new believer to give his or her testimony in a public setting. Nearly four out of the ten churches studied mandated this testimony before a committee or the entire church body.

The issue was often described with a biblical precedent. There were many respondents who believed that the early church in the New Testament required a "tongue confession" of the lordship of Christ. Said an Oklahoma pastor: "Too many so-called new believers (I'm not sure they are really Christians) are never asked to state publicly that Jesus is their Savior. If they are ashamed to claim Christ, I think Christ would be ashamed to claim them."

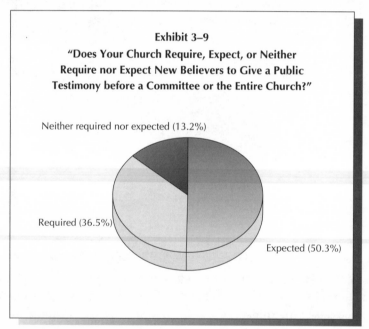

Exhibit 3–9

"Does Your Church Require, Expect, or Neither Require nor Expect New Believers to Give a Public Testimony before a Committee or the Entire Church?"

Neither required nor expected (13.2%)

Required (36.5%)

Expected (50.3%)

Church Covenant

A church covenant is an agreement between the members of a church and the corporate body itself. Though less than 7 percent of the churches required the signing of a covenant as a requirement for membership (another 11 percent expected but did not require signing), mention of this issue is worthy of note. *Where a church covenant was required, retention was extremely effective.* Indeed, the churches with required covenant signings were more than twice as effective in assimilation compared to the other churches in our study.

We received a number of church covenants in our study. Exhibit 3–10 is a verbatim copy from one of the churches. Read it carefully. Then imagine your church requiring its members to sign the document annually and abide by its terms! Most of the churches in our study stated their willingness to enforce some type of church discipline when members persistently neglected or failed to follow the precepts of the covenant.

Two further pieces of data demonstrate the impact of a church covenant. Those churches that used a covenant actively had an attendance virtually equal to their memberships. Second, the average tenure of pastors in these churches was nearly twenty years. "The process of creating accountability through a covenant is painful," one pastor told us. "You really have to have the trust of the people, but even then the resistance is great." This particular pastor began the process after seventeen years of ministry at his church. The adoption of a covenant took nearly another five years.

Truly High-Expectation Churches

Membership in the high-assimilation churches in our study truly means something. Indeed, the members are *expected* to live and minister in a way that is consistent with New Testament precepts. They are expected to attend worship and Sunday School regularly, to adhere to doctrine, to be involved in ministry, to attend new member classes and, if they are new Christians, to be discipled one-on-one, as well as to give a public testimony of their salvation.

Though only a few churches require the signing of a church covenant, those churches that have such a requirement were the most effective in assimilation. But truly all of the high-assimilation churches in our study were high-expectation churches.

The trend is clear. The evidence is staggering. And the results are rewarding. Perhaps one of the most significant church trends in the twenty-first century will be the clear expectations of church members to live for Christ in the context of their local churches. We call them high-expectation churches.

Exhibit 3–10
Sample Church Covenant

Because I am saved by the grace of God through faith in Jesus Christ, a member of the body of Christ and of _____ Baptist Church, with God as my help I agree to do the following:

I agree to read the Bible, meditate upon the Word of God, and pray daily during a planned time.

I agree to pray with and for the members of my household daily, and provide biblical instruction for those under my care.

I agree to regularly attend the worship services at _____ Baptist Church unless hindered by health or circumstances beyond my control (Heb. 10:25).

I agree to abstain from gossip, backbiting, murmuring, and negative talk to or about others (Eph. 4:29).

I agree to respond to personal conflict and disagreement according to Matt. 5:23–24; 18:15–17; Gal. 6:1; Eph. 4:31–32, and other scriptures that govern human relationships.

I agree to regularly and consistently share my faith with others who are unchurched or unsaved and invite them to attend _____ Baptist Church (Matt. 28:18–20).

I agree to regularly participate in a biblical course of study that is consistent with the doctrine that my pastor teaches and preaches.

I agree to be involved in at least one ministry of _____ Baptist Church in order to personally glorify God, edify believers, and persuade sinners to be saved through the ministry of the church.

I agree to give _____ Baptist Church a tenth of my income and additional offerings as God prospers me (Mal. 3:8–11).

I agree to abstain from the use and sale of alcohol as a beverage and from drugs except for medicinal purposes.

I agree to abstain from acts of sexual intimacy with self and any person other than my spouse (1 Thess. 4:3–5).

Foremost I agree to love the Lord my God with all my heart, soul, and might, and to love all others as I love myself (Matt. 22:37–39).

Member Signature _____

Date_____

While these churches may be our twenty-first-century models, they are really following a first-century model. Indeed, the church may eventually look like those early churches in the pages of Scripture where "the number of the disciples continued to increase greatly" (Acts 6:7).

CHAPTER 4

The Pastor and the High-Expectation Church

It scares me to see how much my leadership affects the church.
Pastor in Illinois

God is sovereign. That statement is true theologically and experientially. He is in control of all things, including the churches across our land.

In His sovereignty, God chooses certain means, methods, and persons to accomplish His purpose. And after researching thousands of churches for nearly a decade, I am convinced that one of His primary means of accomplishing His will is through the words, deeds, and leadership of pastors. So much *does* rise and fall on pastoral leaders.

A Profile of Pastors in Growing Churches

Growing churches are adding more members than they lose. Their front doors are more open than their back doors. Their attendance is increasing steadily. Do pastors of these churches have common characteristics? Is there a profile of a "typical pastor of a growing church"?

While the pastors who lead these growing churches certainly are not ministerial clones, they do tend to have common traits. Our research revealed a few such characteristics:

- they are theologically conservative;
- they have longer-than-average tenure in the church they presently serve;
- they are more likely to have attended seminary than not;
- they are usually full-time at their churches;

- they love to preach;
- their preferred preaching style is expository;
- they detest committee meetings and
- they are more visionary than reactionary.

A Pastoral Example

John A. Smith (his real name) is pastor at Oak Grove Baptist Church in Salem, Missouri. When he arrived at the church thirteen years ago, he led the people to see a vision of a church running two thousand in attendance.

A church of two thousand in attendance is significant. But a church of two thousand in attendance in Salem, Missouri, is especially significant, since the population of the town is approximately four thousand.

The pastor had attended a seminary in the Midwest when he came to the church. Oak Grove averaged 75 in attendance upon his arrival. Today attendance is over 400, and 80 or more people are reached for Christ and baptized each year. The church has experienced three major building programs and currently meets in a sanctuary that seats 750.

Pastor Smith describes preaching and the discipling of church members as his most exciting tasks. He estimates that 70 percent of his sermons are expository, and the remaining 30 percent are topical and thematic. He least likes pastoral care and committee meetings.

The change and the growth in the church have come at a price. Numerous families have left the church, and as many as fifty persons simply become inactive each year.

But, as a rule, the members of the church have followed the pastor's leadership gladly. Pastor Smith told us how he leads the church through change. "Usually, I will take an idea or a perceived need to the deacons and get their input early on," he said. "Our church is blessed with exceptional deacons who allow me to do this."

The pastor also seeks creative ideas and input from his members. "Once every two years our church appoints a priorities committee, which is charged with studying the church's needs, both present and short-term," he pointed out. "After making their determinations, they present their findings to the church for revision or approval. I meet with the committees as an advisor and provide any needed information and input."

This model of leadership was common among the pastors of the high-expectation churches. They were willing to cast a vision that only

God could accomplish. Yet they were also willing to seek the advice and counsel of others.

Pastor Smith also provides the leadership for Oak Grove to be a high-expectation church. Though the church does not require the following of new members, they have clear expectations that the people will:

- provide a public testimony of their conversion;
- attend a new member orientation class;
- commit to attend a discipling program;
- commit to spiritual gifts development and eventual service in a ministry of the church;
- tithe;
- attend worship services and Sunday School regularly; and
- commit to follow a specific theological guideline (required).

This expectation model of ministry is not taken lightly at Oak Grove. "If a member has not attended or expressed some support for the church in a six-month period," Pastor Smith said, "they are notified that they are removed from membership."

Most pastors could not survive the implementation of such a policy. But John Smith has built trust over a thirteen-year period. His leadership is trusted and secure. And the church continues to grow.

The Amazing Role of Preaching

In a previous book,[1] I reported on our research of 576 evangelistic churches in America. The most significant finding was the high correlation between expository preaching and evangelistic effectiveness in these churches. The research for the book you are reading demonstrated once again the importance of preaching—this time in closing the back door.

As a reminder, the scale we used to determine assimilation effectiveness was as follows:

1—Not Important at All
2—Only Slightly Important
3—Important
4—Very Important but Not Essential
5—Essential

Remember, Sunday School was the highest-rated methodology with a 4.91 rating. But preaching was rated an amazingly high 4.40.

A pastor in Maryland explained, "My preaching can help close the back door in two ways. First, so many sermons can state clearly the high expectations associated with following Christ." He continued, "But the most important part of preaching is just letting the Word speak for itself. The Holy Spirit will do the work of convicting during the sermon."

Indeed, sermons that are drawn straight from the biblical text were the most common among the pastors in these evangelistic churches. Exhibit 4–1 depicts the definitions we gave of the different preaching styles.

Exhibit 4–1

Definition of Preaching Styles

Expository	Primarily explanation or commentary on the biblical text; expands the central idea of the text; often includes preaching through a book of the Bible.
Topical	Difficult to define; typically a sermon built around a topic with biblical application to that topic.
Thematic	Usually a series of sermons developed around a central theme or idea; does not typically involve preaching through a book of the Bible.
Narrative	Story form that, from the beginning to the end, develops the plot of the story as a theme; a biblical truth in parable form.

We asked the senior pastors of the churches in our study to estimate the percentage of their sermons that reflect each style. Overwhelmingly the expository style of preaching was the dominant approach (see exhibit 4–2).

Pastoral Leadership Styles

Both from the perspective of pastors and the laity we surveyed, one dominant leadership style emerged: high task/high relationship. The four styles from which the pastors and laypersons could choose were:

- High task/high relationship—emphasizes both relationships and "getting things done"; a team captain who participates in the game.
- High task/low relationship—higher interest in production and "getting things done" than in relationships with people; a commander who pushes others to reach goals.

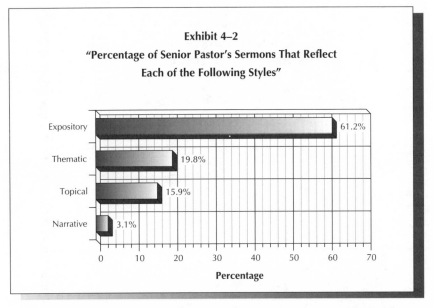

Exhibit 4–2
"Percentage of Senior Pastor's Sermons That Reflect
Each of the Following Styles"

- Low task/high relationship—emphasizes people, feelings, and fellowship more than "getting things done"; a caregiver who primarily ministers to his congregation.
- Low task/low relationship—focuses little on developing relationships or on "getting things done"; a recluse who often retreats from the leadership role.

The self-perceived leadership styles of the pastors were almost always affirmed by laypersons in the churches. A deacon in Georgia, when told that his pastor described himself as "high task/high relationship," responded: "That's a pretty good description of our pastor. He's very goal-oriented, and he's a good people-person as well. Exhibit 4–3 shows the dominance of this approach to leadership by the pastors in the study.

This particular leadership style played an important role as the pastors attempted to lead their churches to change. The "high task" description meant that these men were single-minded in their pursuit to accomplish a goal or task. They had a clear picture of a preferred future, and they did everything they could to see that future become a reality.

But the "high relationship" part of their leadership style meant they cared deeply about people as they attempted to lead the church to change. Though the pastors had an ambitious desire to reach a goal or accomplish

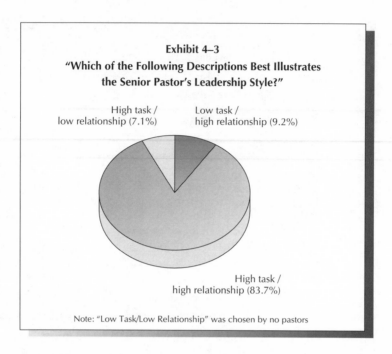

Exhibit 4–3
"Which of the Following Descriptions Best Illustrates
the Senior Pastor's Leadership Style?"

High task /
low relationship (7.1%)

Low task /
high relationship (9.2%)

High task /
high relationship (83.7%)

Note: "Low Task/Low Relationship" was chosen by no pastors

a task, they were unwilling to disregard the concerns of others in the process.

As a consequence, the timing of accomplishing goals was often much longer than the pastors desired. Said an Ohio pastor, "Sometimes I think we can get a new ministry started in two to three months; then I get a surprise!" He continued, "I am tempted just to move ahead without a broad consensus, but I realize that would be a big mistake. So I consult with church leaders and take the time to seek input from the members. The process takes a lot longer, but the end result is healthier."

The Visionary Issue

Vision is a buzzword in both secular and Christian leadership literature. The visionary leader, we are told, will more often than not be successful in the task he sets out to accomplish. So were the pastors visionary? To some extent, it depends upon who answered that question.

We decided to ask the question to four different groups. The first group was comprised of pastors from churches in our original study group.

Remember, these churches were among the most evangelistic churches in the nation. The second group questioned was from these same churches, but this time they were laypersons.

We then asked the same question to pastors and laypersons in nonevangelistic churches. The responses of all four groups were fascinating.

Exhibit 4–4 depicts the range of possible responses on a scale of one to eight. A response of 1 would be the least visionary, while a response of 8 would be the most visionary.

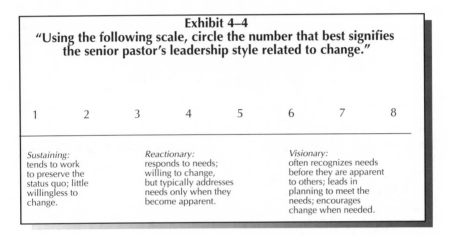

Exhibit 4–4
"Using the following scale, circle the number that best signifies the senior pastor's leadership style related to change."

| 1 | 2 | 3 | 4 | 5 | 6 | 7 | 8 |

Sustaining: tends to work to preserve the status quo; little willingless to change.

Reactionary: responds to needs; willing to change, but typically addresses needs only when they become apparent.

Visionary: often recognizes needs before they are apparent to others; leads in planning to meet the needs; encourages change when needed.

Exhibit 4–5 shows some somewhat surprising results. Pastors in evangelistic churches perceived themselves to be *less* visionary than the laypersons perceived them. But the pastors of the nonevangelistic churches saw themselves as *more* visionary than the laypersons saw them.

The Joys and Pains of the Pastors

The pastors of the churches in our study tend to share some common characteristics. Particularly revealing was their expression of "likes" and "dislikes." And remember as you look at these characteristics of the pastors that these are the leaders of *evangelistic* churches. In our study of assimilation or closing the back door, we only looked at churches that met our evangelistic criteria.

In our survey of the pastors, we asked them to choose the two most exciting aspects of their ministries, as well as the two least exciting.

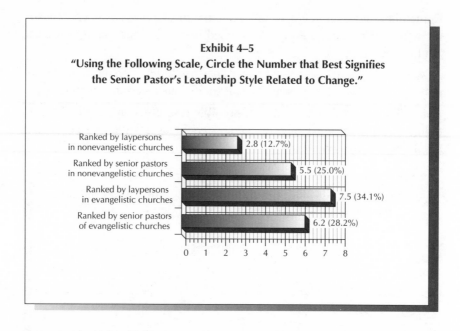

Exhibit 4–5
"Using the Following Scale, Circle the Number that Best Signifies the Senior Pastor's Leadership Style Related to Change."

Ranked by laypersons in nonevangelistic churches — 2.8 (12.7%)
Ranked by senior pastors in nonevangelistic churches — 5.5 (25.0%)
Ranked by laypersons in evangelistic churches — 7.5 (34.1%)
Ranked by senior pastors of evangelistic churches — 6.2 (28.2%)

0 1 2 3 4 5 6 7 8

Their choices were:

- pastoral care,
- preaching,
- administration,
- discipleship/training members,
- personal evangelism,
- building campaigns,
- outreach visitation,
- goal setting,
- committee meetings,
- budgeting,
- future planning, and
- staff leadership.

Several points are noteworthy. First, preaching was by far the most exciting task of these pastors. A pastor in North Carolina articulated his passion: "When someone asks me about my call to ministry, my first response is that I was called to preach. Nothing brings me greater joy than preaching."

The results, in frequency of response, are as follows:

Most Exciting	Least Exciting
1. Preaching (89%)	1. Committee meetings (67%)
2. Personal evangelism (50%)	2. Administration (44%)
3. Pastoral care (26%)	3. Budgeting (34%)
4. Discipleship / training of members (22%)	4. Building campaigns (29%)
5. Outreach visitation (18%)	5. Pastoral care (13%)
6. Future planning (14%)	6. Staff leadership (8%)
7. Goal setting (10%)	7. Goal setting (7%)

Yet it was the joy of preaching that often caused the greatest frustration. A California pastor noted: "If I am to do a credible job in sermon preparation, I need twenty or more hours a week in large blocks of time. But I struggle to make it work. The telephone rings. A crisis hits. Someone has to see me immediately."

Still the pastors of these evangelistic churches somehow find the time to spend significant hours in sermon preparation. Indeed, the time spent in sermon preparation by pastors was one of the most distinguishing characteristics of the evangelistic churches.

We asked a large sample of pastors from our study group to estimate the average amount of time they spent in sermon preparation each week per sermon. We also asked an equal number of pastors from churches which would not meet our evangelistic criteria. As exhibit 4–6 depicts, the contrast is stark.

The pastors from our study group of evangelistic churches spent *five times* more time in sermon preparation compared to the pastors in the nonevangelistic churches. We also found a strong relationship between assimilation and sermon preparation time.

Pastors in the evangelistic churches would therefore spend as many as thirty hours per week, on the average, in sermon preparation time, depending upon the number of different sermons preached. They are willing to take the criticism for their failure to be at every activity, meeting, or ministry need. They truly believe that their time in God's Word is of critical importance; and they believe that the people of God are more than able to

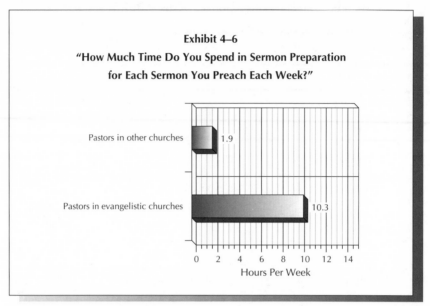

Exhibit 4–6

"How Much Time Do You Spend in Sermon Preparation for Each Sermon You Preach Each Week?"

Pastors in other churches — 1.9

Pastors in evangelistic churches — 10.3

Hours Per Week

do "the work of service, to the building up of the body of Christ" (Eph. 4:12).

These pastors referred often to Acts 6:1–7, particularly the words of the apostolic twelve who said: "It is not desirable for us to neglect the word of God in order to serve tables" (Acts 6:2). They understood fully that if the ministry of the church depended solely upon them, ministry would never get done. Indeed, they echoed the apostles' words, "But we will devote ourselves to prayer, and to the ministry of the word" (Acts 6:4).

But the pastors in the nonevangelistic churches allowed themselves to get distracted in other tasks. They were more likely to give in to the pressure to be omnipresent. And still others did indicate that they had the same sense of passion and calling to a preaching ministry.

Another noteworthy revelation in the "most exciting" category was the evangelistic pastors' love of personal evangelism. Half of the pastors in our study indicated that personal evangelism was one of their two most exciting tasks. They set the standard for sharing Christ, and they expected the members to share a similar zeal.

Pastoral care was a task named in the top five of both the "most exciting" and "least exciting" lists. Approximately one out of four pastors in the study told us they truly found fulfillment in hospital ministry, counseling, funerals, weddings, and other similar pastoral ministries.

But 13 percent of the pastors called pastoral care their least exciting task. I would have placed myself in this latter group. Church members often told me that, after spending time with me as the counselor, they usually felt worse!

Another interesting comparison is that of the "likes" of pastors in evangelistic churches versus the "likes" of pastors in churches that did not meet the evangelistic criteria. Nearly nine out of ten of the evangelistic pastors selected preaching as one of their passions, but only four out of ten pastors in the nonevangelistic churches did so (exhibit 4–7).

Churches with evangelistic pastors usually become evangelistic. The people of the church follow their pastor's leadership. It is no surprise then that the pastors in the evangelistic churches rated personal evangelism as one of their two most exciting tasks.

Exhibit 4–7
"What Tasks Do You Find Most Exciting in Pastoral Ministry?"

Pastors in Evangelistic Churches	Pastors in Other Churches
1. Preaching (89%)	1. Pastoral care (71%)
2. Personal evangelism (50%)	2. Preaching (41%)
3. Pastoral care (26%)	3. Administration (19%)
4. Discipleship/training members (22%)	4. Committee meetings (16%)
5. Outreach visitation (18%)	5. Discipleship/training members (15%)

Committee meetings were the most despised tasks of the pastors in evangelistic churches. Two out of three of these pastors expressed a great deal of frustration with their churches' committee system. Said a Louisiana pastor: "Most of our committees meet just to meet. They exist because they've always existed. They really don't accomplish much."

Interestingly, among the pastors in the nonevangelistic churches, one out of six called committee meetings one of their two most exciting tasks. The meetings ranked fourth in their favorite endeavors.

The pastors are not monolithic in their likes and dislikes, but a clear pattern emerged. The pastors of the evangelistic churches are much more likely to have a passion for preaching and personal evangelism.

Who (or What) Influences the Pastors?

We asked the pastors to rate the level of influence of different factors in their development as a leader. The scale we used was:

1. Not an influence

2. A slight influence

3. An important influence

4. A very important influence

5. A most significant influence

Many of the pastors in the evangelistic churches cited their own experiences as the most important factor in their leadership development. An Arkansas pastor explained, "Nothing has been a better teacher for me than actual experience. Seminary helped, but 'the school of hard knocks' was the best leadership teacher."

Exhibit 4–8 shows the relative level of influence of different factors in leadership development. Actual experience and mentor examples were the highest rated responses.

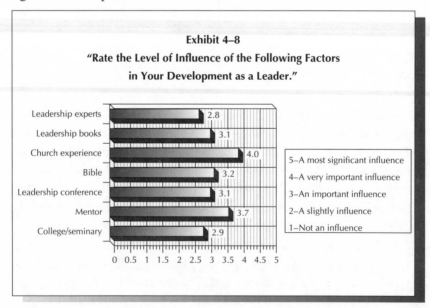

Exhibit 4–8

"Rate the Level of Influence of the Following Factors in Your Development as a Leader."

Factor	Rating
Leadership experts	2.8
Leadership books	3.1
Church experience	4.0
Bible	3.2
Leadership conference	3.1
Mentor	3.7
College/seminary	2.9

5–A most significant influence
4–A very important influence
3–An important influence
2–A slightly influence
1–Not an influence

Pastors in High-Expectation Churches

For most of this chapter, we have been examining the characteristics of pastors in evangelistic churches. But our study was primarily concerned with assimilation. When we divided the churches in our study into the higher-assimilation churches versus the lower-assimilation churches, we found several traits that were *more* prominent in pastors in higher-assimilation churches.

The Expository Preaching Issue

Pastors in the higher-assimilation churches were much more likely to give their preaching styles as expository. Indeed, they often viewed their expository messages as vehicles for communicating the high expectation of following Christ. And, congruent with the main thesis of our study, high expectations led to higher assimilation.

The Pastoral Care Issue

These pastors were less likely to find pastoral care an exciting ministry than their counterparts in lower-assimilation churches. They were quicker to delegate or ask laypersons to do ministry. They were also willing to accept the criticisms that are common when pastors are not present at every function or ministry need.

Their Attitude toward the Church

Pastors of the higher-assimilation churches tended to have a positive attitude toward the churches they served. When asked how their church typically responds to a challenge to change, they would describe the response as "open to change as long as study, prayer, and leadership support the need to change." And even if change came with difficulty, the pastors described the congregations as willing to follow but at a slower pace.

Other pastors tended to be more pessimistic about their churches. They described the people as "reluctant to change" and stated that changes come "grudgingly only when forced by circumstances."

A Concern for Disciple Making

The pastors in the high-assimilation churches were evangelistic, but they desired to see more than converts to Christ. Their passion was to see "fruit-bearing disciples" for Christ. While they rejoiced in every decision that was made, they were not satisfied until the new Christian was demonstrating clear evidence of his or her salvation.

That desire to see disciples more than converts led the pastors to be much more intentional about the assimilation process. Indeed, even while evangelistic efforts were being made, discipleship issues were not ignored.

Thus, because of the pastoral leadership in the higher-assimilation churches, evangelism and discipleship were not polarized into distinct or separate categories. The process of evangelism continued without interruption into the process of discipleship.

If any single word could describe the pastors in the high-assimilation churches, it would be *intentional*. They are intentionally evangelistic, and they are intentional about assimilation. Their congregations are not unaware of the pastors' commitments, so they are likely to follow his example. The result is a church reaching many for Christ and retaining them in active ministry. And the result is therefore a high-expectation church, the theme which we will continue into the next chapter.

CHAPTER 5

How Prospects Are Treated and Evangelized

> On our first visit to the church, we felt like we had found a home.
>
> Visitor to one of the churches in our study

The experience of interviewing visitors to the churches in our study was one of the most rewarding aspects of our research. We were able to see beyond the statistics and responses to a "real life" encounter with people whose lives had been touched by people in these churches.

Travel with me to the beautiful state of Florida (always one of my favorite places to conduct on-site interviews). In this portion of the state is a church that has seen its attendance double in three years. And most of the growth has come from conversion growth.

With permission from the pastor, I wait for someone to return to their car in the guest parking space after the morning worship service. Since the first family to arrive has a screaming toddler, I elect to wait on someone else. Within minutes a nice-looking young couple, probably in their early to mid-twenties, returns to their car.

I introduce myself, tell them of my purpose for visiting the church that day, and ask them if they could spare a few minutes. They graciously agree.

My primary interest, I explain, is to learn how they were received and treated from the moment they arrived on the church campus to their departure. Their story is fascinating.

"We usually don't visit a Sunday School class the first time we visit a church," Ed explained, "but we were frustrated." Melanie continued the conversation, "Ed and I have visited about ten different churches since we moved here. Though none of the churches were bad experiences, we just weren't connecting with the people. So we decided to visit a Sunday School class first this time."

Melanie was eager to continue: "We weren't very comfortable about going to a Sunday School class. You know how it is. You don't know anyone. You can't find the class. You don't have a clue what they will be teaching. We were really uneasy."

Ed interjected, "It didn't take long to put our fears at rest. When we got out of our car, we were met by two nice gentlemen who had name tags identifying themselves as greeters. One of them asked if he could take us into the building."

Ed continued, "They took us to a welcome center, which was just a table with a nice tablecloth. Three people were standing at the table. We were introduced to all three of them."

"One of them really took the initiative with us," Melanie said. "She asked questions so that she could recommend a Sunday School class to us. When we found a class that seemed to fit us, she actually took us to the classroom. That really blew me away. She actually took us there herself!"

But the surprises did not end there. Melanie continued the story: "When we arrived at the Sunday School class, a couple met us at the door. They talked with us and introduced us to others. Then they sat with us during the Sunday School."

"The biggest surprise," Ed offered, "was that the couple asked if they could sit with us during the worship service. We just left them a few minutes before we got here. They've invited us to lunch next Sunday."

My question had such an obvious answer that I hesitated to ask.

Would they return?

"Absolutely," said Ed.

"We've found a home!" Melanie exclaimed.

Profile of a Prospect

The events in the Florida church were not coincidental. The church had a well-organized greeter ministry. Even the greeters in the Sunday School class are trained to sit with visitors and to ask to sit with them in worship services. And the church offers to reimburse any member who takes a first-time guest to lunch.

In the evangelistic churches we studied, slightly over 5 percent of those in attendance were first-time guests. That number may not seem high, but the cumulative impact over several weeks is significant. A church averaging two hundred in attendance with 5 percent first-time guests will have over five hundred first-time visitors in a year.

Exhibit 5–1 shows the makeup of a Sunday morning worship attendance. Since some categories are not mutually exclusive, the numbers will not add to 100 percent.

Exhibit 5–1

"Average Percentage of Sunday Morning Worship Attenders Who Are. . . ."

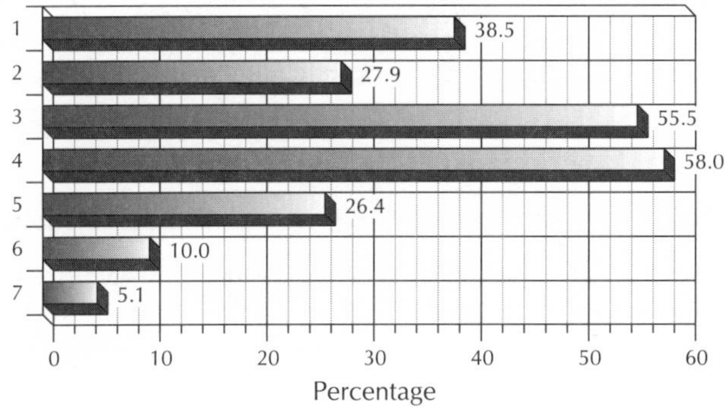

1. Church members who attend Sunday School and worship regulary, hold a position, and financially support the church
2. Church members who hold a position or task in the church
3. Church members who attend Sunday School and worship 50% of the time
4. Church members who attend more than 50% of services
5. Church members who attend less than 50% of services
6. Regular attenders/Not members
7. First-time guests

When guests come to one of the churches in our study, the statistical probability of their returning for a second visit is better than six out of ten. The higher-assimilation churches in our study, however, had a significantly higher frequency of return visits than that of the lower-assimilation churches.

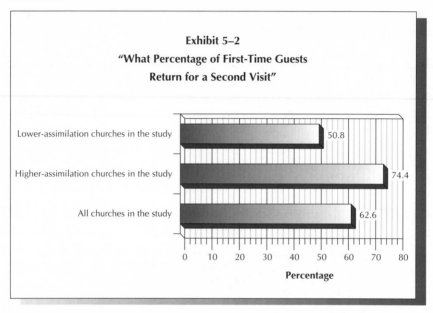

Exhibit 5–2
"What Percentage of First-Time Guests
Return for a Second Visit"

Lower-assimilation churches in the study — 50.8

Higher-assimilation churches in the study — 74.4

All churches in the study — 62.6

0   10   20   30   40   50   60   70   80

Percentage

Exhibit 5–2 shows that churches with a more effective assimilation process are more likely to see first-time guests return for at least a second visit. How does assimilation relate to guest retention? Apparently, the response to that question can best be summarized by the word *expectations*. Listen to some of the comments by visitors at the high-assimilation churches.

- "Unlike some other churches we visited, this church seemed to act like the Christian faith really mattered."
- "We were met by greeters everywhere we turned. We never lost our way. It's easy to see that this church expects a lot of its members."
- "This church has a reputation in town for making a difference. After one visit I can sense what everyone is saying."
- "Everything about the church told me that the people cared, that they took their faith seriously."

The theme of high expectations runs through our study and consequently through this book. But we were somewhat surprised to learn that first-time guests to the church were able to articulate that same theme. They could really discern if the people in the church were people of low or high commitment.

The high-expectation churches affected the guests in at least two ways. First, the visitors sensed that God was "up to something" at these churches, that the churches were really making a difference. The visitors thus desired to return to a place where God was obviously at work.

Second, the guests who began steps toward church membership understood clearly that they would not be joining a church where they could fade into anonymity. They knew that ministry and service would be expected of them. In some ways, then, the prospective members were already being assimilated into the church before they joined. They knew involvement was not an option.

The Motivation for the First Visit

What made the visitors come to the church in the first place? Exhibit 5–3 illustrates the obvious response. A friend or family member or coworker invited the guest. For many years church growth pundits have advocated this "relationship invitation" and, indeed, our statistics confirm earlier studies.

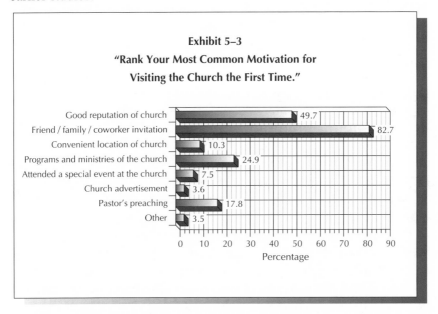

Exhibit 5–3
"Rank Your Most Common Motivation for
Visiting the Church the First Time."

Good reputation of church — 49.7
Friend / family / coworker invitation — 82.7
Convenient location of church — 10.3
Programs and ministries of the church — 24.9
Attended a special event at the church — 7.5
Church advertisement — 3.6
Pastor's preaching — 17.8
Other — 3.5

Percentage

When we asked the guests to rank their most common motivations for visiting a church for the first time, over 80 percent ranked an invitation by a friend, family member, or coworker either first or second. Other responses were distant in comparison.

While other studies have rightly demonstrated the vital importance of inviting people to church, they have failed to articulate why some churches are much more successful at relationship invitation than others.

As I write this chapter, I am in St. Louis, where I just returned from speaking at a conference. After the conference I met with a pastor from a town in Missouri about two hours from St. Louis. His story is not uncommon.

"For years I've heard that the way to grow your church is to get your members to invite their friends and acquaintances. So I've pleaded with my church for a long time to invite people they know." He continued, "Most of the members nod politely but never invite anyone. And the few who do invite people get discouraged because their friends rarely return. What's our problem?"

In chapter 2 you read about the critical importance of Sunday School. Yet you also read that the mere existence of a Sunday School does not automatically close the back door. The quality of the organization, the evangelistic intentionality, and the level of accountability are all critical factors that determine the effectiveness of Sunday School in the assimilation of members.

Likewise, the mere act of inviting is insufficient. What other studies have failed to communicate is the *motive* behind inviting and the *motive* behind the responses to the invitations. Some writers have indicated that the primary issue is worship style. As one pastor shared with me, "I can't ask my people to invite generation Xers and Baby Boomers to a worship service straight from the 1950s."

But even those who insist that worship styles must change are not fully seeing the motivation behind relationship invitation. Indeed, we found no correlation between worship style and evangelistic effectiveness in an earlier study.[1]

The deeper issue behind effective relationship invitations is the commitment level of the church. If people in the church believe their fellowship is making a difference for the kingdom, they will be enthusiastic about inviting their friends to church. Likewise, if visitors sense that the church is making a difference, then they will be eager to be a part of it.

That is why the reputation of the church was second in motivations given for visiting a church (see exhibit 5–3). Most people desire to be a part of something that is making a difference. Members invite eagerly, and guests respond enthusiastically.

Though the words at this point may sound redundant, the issue is still one of high expectations. Churches that expect much of their people typically receive much. Churches where people eagerly give of their time and ministry typically make a difference. And churches that make a difference have members who are excited about sharing their churches with others.

The Greeter Issue

Another surprising aspect of our study was the importance of a greeter ministry. And again, at the risk of further redundancy, we must emphasize that the mere existence of a greeter ministry is not adequate.

First, we must determine how a greeter ministry affects guests and ultimately impacts the assimilation effectiveness of the church. The issue is important especially in view of the strong correlation between a greeter ministry and high assimilation.

Exhibit 5–4 shows that the vast majority of the churches in our study had some type of greeter ministry. Since our first study group was only evangelistic churches, we can assume that there was some correlation between effective evangelism and the greeter ministry.

But churches that were effective in *both* their evangelism *and* assimilation were more likely to have an organized greeter ministry. Exhibit 5a and 5b show that 98.3 percent of the evangelistic and higher-assimilation churches had a greater ministry, compared to 85.5 percent of the lower-assimilation churches.

How, then, can there be a relationship between a greeter ministry and assimilation? From our postsurvey interviews, it seems that the issue of high expectations once again explains the more effective assimilation. The greeter ministry communicates to guests and prospective members that the church has high expectations of its members, that the members really do desire to make a difference. The prospective member senses that if he or she joins the church, much will be expected of him or her as well. The member thus comes to the church anticipating that anonymity is not an option.

As strange as it may seem, our research *does* indicate that an effective greeter ministry enhances the assimilation process. The "front door" issue

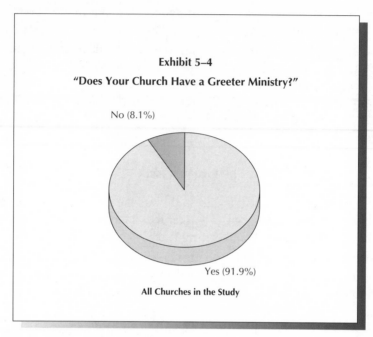

Exhibit 5–4

"Does Your Church Have a Greeter Ministry?"

No (8.1%)

Yes (91.9%)

All Churches in the Study

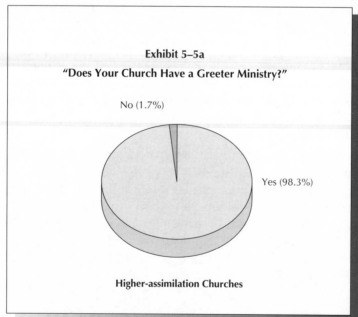

Exhibit 5–5a

"Does Your Church Have a Greeter Ministry?"

No (1.7%)

Yes (98.3%)

Higher-assimilation Churches

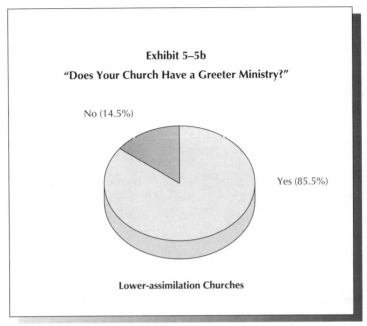

Exhibit 5–5b
"Does Your Church Have a Greeter Ministry?"

No (14.5%)

Yes (85.5%)

Lower-assimilation Churches

of greeting guests has profound implications for the "back door" issue of retaining members in active service.

Since the greeter ministry has implications for assimilation, what other issues did our research uncover? Some of the interesting factors related to the greeter ministry included the following:

- Visitors strongly preferred that greeters wear name tags that identified them and their ministry. The guests were much more likely to seek assistance from persons with clear identification.

- Greeters in our study churches were positioned in numerous areas throughout the church campus. Less than 35 percent of the study churches had greeters at the front door only.

- Nearly three out of ten churches had greeters in the parking lot. But the visitors were adamant that these greeters refrain from any attempts to open their car doors. (One visitor feared that his car was about to be hijacked!)

- Over half of the churches had greeters at all entrance doors.

- Over 35 percent of the churches had a welcome center. The most common welcome center was a table covered by a nice tablecloth.

- Nearly three-fourths of the churches had greeters in the worship services.
- Fifty-four percent of the churches had greeters in the Sunday School classes. In the majority of the churches, the primary role of these greeters was to sit with visitors during Sunday School, to accompany them to the worship service, and to offer to sit with them again in worship.

How Are Visitors Identified in Worship Services?

Churches that effectively assimilate their members recognize guests in worship services in four basic ways, although one approach was dominant. The approaches are given below in reverse order of frequency.

Least Used: No Formal Recognition

Only 3 percent of the churches in our study made no attempt to identify their visitors. These few churches depended upon the staff's and member's ability to remember guests' names, if any attempt was made at all. The lack of formal recognition was the result of the church leadership's desire not to put a visitor on the spot, to make him or her uncomfortable.

But the very small number using this approach reflects the desire of most churches to know who visited on a given Sunday (or in a few exceptions, worship days other than Sunday). These church leaders realized that follow-up was critical and that follow-up was impossible without names.

Second Least Used: Visitors Remain Seated While Members Stand

Only one in seven of our study churches asked members to stand while the guests remained seated. While this method typically identifies visitors easily, it has relatively low support because of the perceived discomfort for the visitors. And, as a minister of education in Georgia told us, "The view is not too good for the visitors during the welcome time."

Third Least Used: Guests Raise Hands

About one in six churches ask the visitors to raise their hands during a welcome time. This method is not used frequently because of both low response rates and the perception that visitors are put on the spot.

Exhibit 5–6
Sample Registration Card

Welcome to

Date _____

Dr./Rev./Ms.

Mr./Mrs/Miss. _____   Phone (   ) _____

Address _____ Apt._____   Wk. Phone _____

City _____ State_____   Zip _____

Is This Your . . .

❏ First Time? I came as a guest of _____

❏ Second Time? ❏ Third Time?   ❏ Attender   ❏Member

Present Church Membership _____

Your School Grade	**Or Age Group**	**Please Circle:**
K 1 2 3 4 5 6 7 8	18–29 30–35 36–40 41–45	Single
9 10 11 12 College	46–49 50–55 56–64 65–66+	Married

Names of your childred living at home: Birthday:

_____

_____

(Please see other side)

- -

I'd like information on:

❏ How to become a Christian
❏ Next Membership Class
❏ Spiritual growth
❏ Teacher training
❏ Missions
❏ Adult Bible study
❏ Music activities
❏ Singles activities
❏ College activities
❏ Youth activities
❏ Preschool children activities
❏ Prayer needs:

I would like to:

❏ Commit my life to Christ
❏ Renew my commitment to Christ
❏ Be baptized
❏ Be enrolled in next membership class
❏ Help where needed
❏ Enroll in Sunday School
❏ Join the church
❏ Reservations for Wed. night dinner

_____

_____

_____

Would you like a prayergram sent to the person prayed for?

❏ Yes ❏ No. If Yes, provide address.

_____

_____

(Please see other side)

Most Frequently Used: Everyone Completes a Registration Card

Well over half of the study churches asked everyone present in the worship service to fill out a registration card. Members typically put their name only on the card; some of them may provide information such as prayer requests or a willingness to be involved in a ministry.

The visitors present are thus not singled out; everyone is writing on a registration card. From the data we received, this method of recognizing guests is growing in popularity. An example of one of these cards is shown in exhibit 5–6.

The Issue of Visitor Follow-Up

Though some church growth pundits have indicated that visitor follow-up is not welcome in today's culture, our research indicates that it is critical for both growth and ultimately retention. While a few churches can boast of dynamic growth with little follow-up outreach, their examples are rare. And, unfortunately, many church leaders have followed those examples with disastrous results in their own churches.

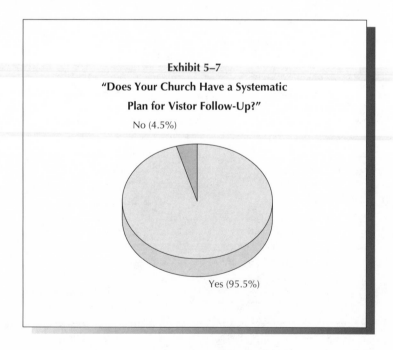

Exhibit 5–7
"Does Your Church Have a Systematic
Plan for Vistor Follow-Up?"
No (4.5%)

Yes (95.5%)

Because all of our study churches were evangelistic churches, our research team knew that their responses to the issue of visitor follow-up would be revealing. Perhaps "revealing" was an understatement.

Nearly all of the churches in our study had some well-planned, regular program for visitor follow-up. A pastor in Colorado discontinued his church's regular outreach, thinking it was ineffective and a poor use of time. "I made a huge mistake," he told us. "When we stopped having regular outreach, the spirit of the church moved from excitement to apathy. I'll never be disobedient to the Great Commission again!"

Perhaps even more revealing was that 99.1 percent of the high-assimilation churches had a systematic plan for visitor follow-up. As exhibit 5–8 seems to indicate, regular outreach affected both the number of new members added *and* the retention of those members.

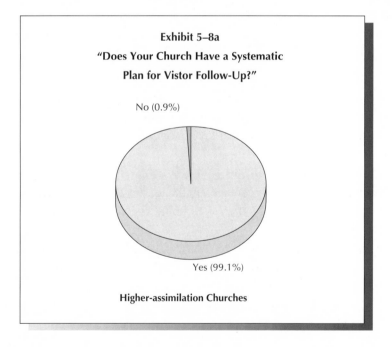

Exhibit 5–8a

"Does Your Church Have a Systematic Plan for Vistor Follow-Up?"

No (0.9%)

Yes (99.1%)

Higher-assimilation Churches

Though the survey data is descriptive, what is more revealing is to visit these churches and to sense the commitment level to outreach. The leaders of these churches would not think of neglecting those who visited their churches. And in a day when personal visits are deemed archaic, offensive,

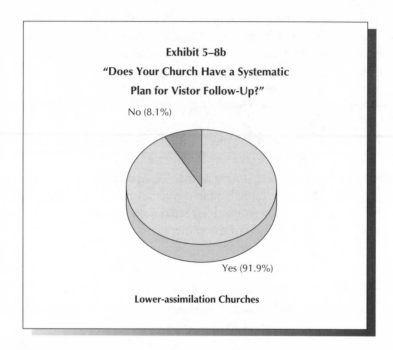

Exhibit 5–8b

"Does Your Church Have a Systematic

Plan for Vistor Follow-Up?"

No (8.1%)

Yes (91.9%)

Lower-assimilation Churches

insensitive, and ineffective, almost every church in our study had either the pastor, other staff member, or a layperson visit the person or guest who came to the church.

Exhibit 5–9 depicts the different ways churches conducted a visitor follow-up. And as the percentages indicate, most churches had multiple forms of follow-up. Clearly the day of home visitation is not dead in evangelistic churches.

Some observations about the visitor follow-up of these churches may be noteworthy. They seem to go against much of the conventional church growth wisdom of today.

- Almost every church insisted on personal visit follow-up by the pastor, other staff, or a layperson.
- Higher-assimilation churches were more likely to deliver a "gift" as the first step in their visitor follow-up.
- A visit from a layperson (almost seven out of ten visitor follow-ups in these churches is lay led) was deemed most effective by the visitors we interviewed.

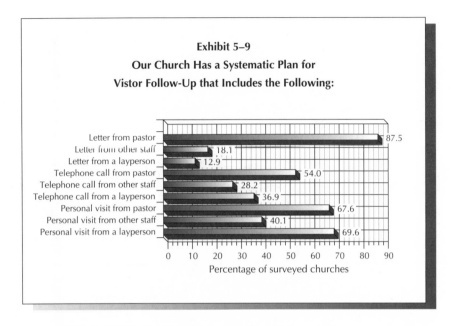

Exhibit 5–9

**Our Church Has a Systematic Plan for
Vistor Follow-Up that Includes the Following:**

- Sensitivity to time and convenience of the prospects were emphasized in most of these churches; those involved in visitor follow-up
  rarely heard complaints about intrusion from the visitors.

- The average number of "contacts" (telephone, visit, letter, etc.) was
  four in the first week after a guest visited the church.

- The visitors were more impressed with a visit from a layperson than
  from the pastor. The pastor was still involved, however, in personal
  visits in 67.6 percent of the churches studied. But, according to the
  visitors to these churches, they would be satisfied with just a letter
  from the pastor.

Frequency of visitor follow-up was determinative for those guests to
return for at least a second time. Those churches that had a regular weekly
outreach had a higher visitor return rate than the churches with outreach on
a less frequent basis, and exhibit 5–10 shows that more than eight out of
ten of the study churches had a plan for weekly outreach.

Those churches that have a regular and established time for their visitor
follow-up outnumbered other churches in the study by more than a
three-to-one ratio. And our research team continued to find a positive relationship between "front door" methods and "back door" results. In the

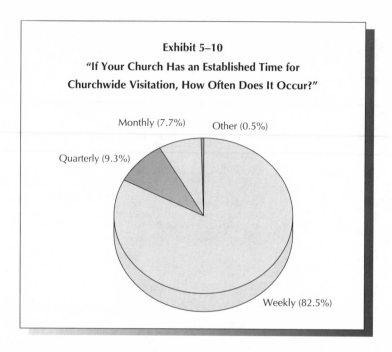

Exhibit 5–10

"If Your Church Has an Established Time for Churchwide Visitation, How Often Does It Occur?"

Monthly (7.7%)   Other (0.5%)

Quarterly (9.3%)

Weekly (82.5%)

aggregate, the churches in exhibit 5–11 that responded "yes" had a significantly higher retention rate than those that responded "no."

Was a particular *day* for outreach more effective than others? Much to our surprise, our data answers that question with a resounding "yes." First, for the churches with an established time for outreach, what particular day did they use?

As we focused on particular days for outreach, we were again surprised that visitation on two days of the week seemed to be much more effective than others. The most frequent days of outreach were Monday and Tuesday. But the most effective days of outreach were Sunday and Monday. Though we cannot with certainty understand all the implications, *we found that Sunday and Monday outreach resulted in a much higher visitor return rate than any other days of the week.* This relationship seemed so profound that we dubbed it the "thirty-six-hour principle": *If a person visits your church for the first time, the probability of their returning a second time is considerably higher if you make contact with them within thirty-six hours of their visit.*

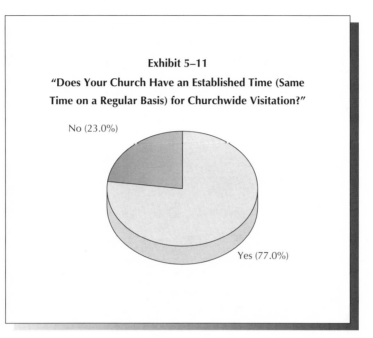

Exhibit 5–11

"Does Your Church Have an Established Time (Same Time on a Regular Basis) for Churchwide Visitation?"

No (23.0%)

Yes (77.0%)

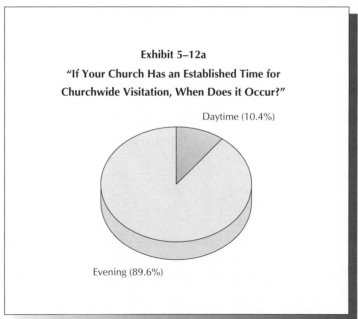

Exhibit 5–12a

"If Your Church Has an Established Time for Churchwide Visitation, When Does it Occur?"

Daytime (10.4%)

Evening (89.6%)

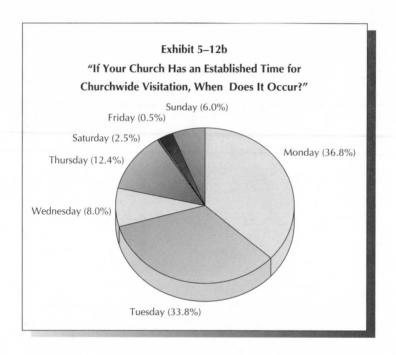

Exhibit 5–12b

"If Your Church Has an Established Time for Churchwide Visitation, When Does It Occur?"

Sunday (6.0%)
Friday (0.5%)
Saturday (2.5%)
Thursday (12.4%)
Monday (36.8%)
Wednesday (8.0%)
Tuesday (33.8%)

The Parking Surprise

We were anticipating that nearly all of the evangelistic churches in our study would have specific parking spaces for guests. To our surprise, only 56.5 percent of the respondents indicated that their churches had visitor parking. In our follow-up interviews we found no single explanation for this enigma. The responses were varied. Below is a sampling of the responses.

- "Our members save the closer parking spaces for senior adults, families with small children, and guests. We don't have to mark designated spaces."
- "We found that a few people became 'perpetual guests' just to get a good parking space, so we did away with the spaces."
- "Our church is rural; the people are as likely to park on the grass rather than the few paved spots we have."
- "We did a study on parking at our church and found that three-fourths of the guests weren't using designated parking anyway."
- "We were told by many guests that they were uncomfortable parking in designated places."

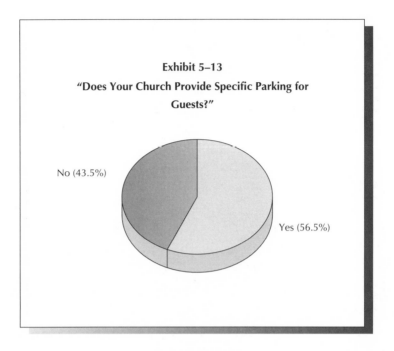

Exhibit 5–13
"Does Your Church Provide Specific Parking for Guests?"

No (43.5%)

Yes (56.5%)

Guest Seating?

Less than 5 percent of our study churches had specific seating for guests. In fact, we were so curious about the few that did provide guest seating that we telephoned some of the churches. An associate pastor in Florida gave us a common response: "We don't actually have signs that say 'guest seating.' Your survey question asked if we reserved specific seating for guests. We answered 'yes' because we have trained our members to fill up the front seating first. So when visitors come in, they don't have to walk in front of everyone to find a seat."

Conclusion: Churches with an Outward Focus

Our research team over the past four years has studied hundreds of churches across our nation. As we researched evangelistic churches, we found a certain atmosphere of expectancy, an intangible that cannot be measured with data and statistics. We found churches whose focus was ever outward, whose desire to obey the Great Commission was intense.

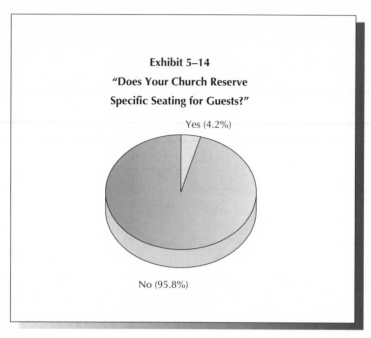

Exhibit 5–14
"Does Your Church Reserve
Specific Seating for Guests?"

Yes (4.2%)

No (95.8%)

We also found that these churches were not laissez faire in their attitudes toward evangelism and assimilation. To the contrary, they were highly intentional about reaching and retaining people. Hardly a day would go by in these churches where the leaders were not examining some aspect of their outward focus. *Intentionality* is one word that describes these churches well.

Another descriptive word for the outward focus of these churches would be *organized*. These churches were not haphazard in their methodologies to reach out to those who visited them. Indeed, for many of the churches, their level of efficiency and organization was nothing less than remarkable. The leaders of these churches were determined that no one would "fall through the cracks" because of sloppy organization.

But the word that describes these churches repeatedly in our study is *expectations*. They expect their fellowship to be friendly. They expect their members to be involved in outreach ministries. They expect the people to have a passion to reach the lost and to disciple and assimilate new members and new Christians.

Though the process can seem painfully slow at times, they are persistent. Ultimately, because they expect much, they receive much. They become churches that make a difference. And prospects quickly discover that they want to be a part of a church that makes a difference. Thus, it is no great mystery why the churches in our study are growing and retaining their growth. They are truly high-expectation churches.

CHAPTER 6

Expectations Clarified:
The New Member Class

Over half of the conversions in our church come through our new member class.

Associate Pastor in Florida

"Dr. Rainer," the young pastor asked, "is there any one thing that distinguishes churches that close the back door from other churches?" My first impression the initial time I heard this question was that the pastor was looking for an easy answer to a complex situation. I imagined him to be the type of leader who would always look for the easiest way to minister, regardless of its effectiveness. I soon discovered how wrong I was.

The pastor's question was sincere. He was frustrated with losing members or seeing active members lose their zeal for ministry. He estimated that he lost 10 percent of his congregation to inactivity or transfer to other churches every year.

As church leaders around the nation learned that we were doing this research project, I began to receive literally hundreds of inquiries. "What," they asked, "can we do to stop the loss of members?"

Not anxious to reveal material not fully assembled and interpreted, I was willing to share only a limited amount of information. So I told them about the critical importance of Sunday School, the material you read in chapter 1. And the response was gratifying. So many churches that contacted us began to review their Sunday Schools; many made significant changes to help their Sunday Schools make a difference in the lives of people.

But questions persisted. Were there any genuine surprises? Were there any "discoveries"? Were there any innovative ministries that made a difference in the assimilation process?

Though at the time I did not have all of the information you will read in this chapter, I am now confident of the "new discovery." One of the key issues in closing the back door was the presence of a new member class as a required entry point for members.

To understand more fully the significance of a new member class, look at the responses of three categories of churches to a question regarding the new member class:

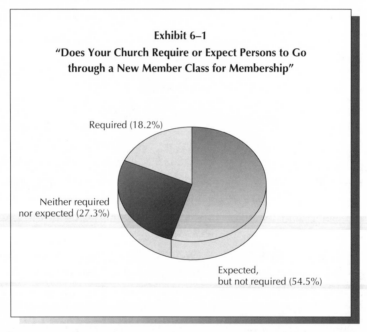

Exhibit 6–1
"Does Your Church Require or Expect Persons to Go through a New Member Class for Membership"

Required (18.2%)

Neither required nor expected (27.3%)

Expected, but not required (54.5%)

The pie exhibit shown in 6–1 needs to be examined closely. Over half of the churches have expectations that persons complete a new member class for membership, but they do *not* require it. Slightly over 18 percent *require* a membership class as an entry point. But over one fourth of the churches neither require nor expect attendance in a membership class.

Can the New Member Class Help Close the Back Door?

How important is the new member class in the retention of members? Exhibit 6–2 is revealing.

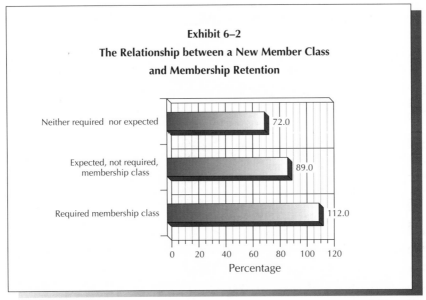

Exhibit 6–2

The Relationship between a New Member Class
and Membership Retention

Though this study cannot draw dogmatic conclusions, the relationship between assimilation effectiveness and new member classes is amazing. Our research team examined the retention level of the new members over a two-year period. As exhibit 6-2 indicates, churches that *require* persons to enter membership through a new member class have a much higher retention rate than those that do not.

To understand our concept of retention rate, an example might be in order. A church in Oklahoma had 300 in average attendance in 1995. During 1996 the church added 45 new members, but the average attendance increased to 360 by the end of the year. In other words the attendance increased at a pace *greater* than the number of new members. We would interpret this church to have a retention rate above 100 percent. For those who desire to see our precise calculation of this ratio, I encourage you to read the note at the end of this book.[1]

Now note the retention rate of churches that require a new member class. They are actually experiencing a growth greater than the number of new members added each year. The churches that encourage or expect, but do not require, persons to attend a membership class have a retention rate of 89 percent. This rate is lower than the 112 percent rate of the required-membership-class churches but healthy nevertheless.

The evangelistic churches that neither require nor expect members to attend a new member class had a retention rate of 72 percent over two years.

How does a new member class impact the assimilation rate of churches? The question is best answered by the theme of this book and research project—high expectations. In simplest terms, churches tend to receive in commitment what they expect from the new members when they join.

A church that communicates no expectations or commitment levels is much more likely to lose members to transfer or inactivity than a high-expectation church. Such has been the thesis of this book and our research project. But what relationship exists between new member classes and high-expectation churches?

In our postsurvey interview we discovered that one of the critical points to communicate expectations is at the point prior to a person's becoming a member of a church. "Frontend" requirements or expectations were deemed to be much more effective than the communication of expectations later in their tenure. And the new member class, more than any other venue, was the vehicle by which expectations were most effectively communicated.

Now please refer back to exhibit 6–2. Churches that *require* membership class attendance *prior* to membership have significantly higher retention rates than other churches. Yet, as exhibit 6–1 indicates, less than one out of five churches do require a membership class as a point of entry. Why are such a relatively small number of churches using such an effective tool? The responses we were given largely fell into two categories.

The first category was change resistance, the we've-never-done-it-that-way-before syndrome. We were surprised to hear of the level of opposition to required membership classes by laypersons in many churches. A pastor in Texas told us: "I couldn't believe the fuss my members caused. One deacon told me that it was unchristian and unbiblical to tell people that they have to go through a membership class. He even hinted that I was placing my job at risk by attempting to do so."

Churches that are accustomed to receiving members without any front-end requirements are often resistant to change. They perceive the membership class as legalistic or unfair. Many pastors, therefore, are not yet able to lead their churches to make a change that has such negative perceptions.

A second category of responses came mostly from pastors. These pastors feared that raising the requirement levels for membership would reduce the number of new members added to the church, and this would reduce the church's overall growth rate. Their concerns are partly justified.

A church that begins a new member class as a requirement for membership *does* typically see a reduction in new members added the first one or two years. But that decline is usually reversed after two years. The retention rate, however, is much higher in the church that requires the membership class.

Though we do not have aggregate data on this phenomenon, it was a pattern that we saw repeated numerous times. Perhaps a "reallife" example can demonstrate the effectiveness of the new member class more clearly.

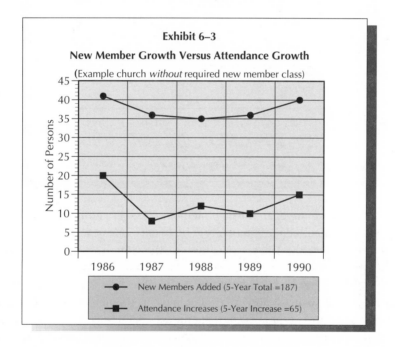

Exhibit 6–3

New Member Growth Versus Attendance Growth

(Example church *without* required new member class)

In the example scenario of exhibit 6–3, a church in Alabama has demonstrated a fairly healthy growth pattern. From 1986 to 1990 the church added 187 new members. The obvious concern with their growth was the much smaller attendance increase over the same period. From 1986 to 1990 the attendance increased by 65, about one-third of the new members added for the same period.

After a year of planning and debating the merits of a new member class, the church finally decided to make the class a requirement for membership. The numerical results after implementing the required class are shown in exhibit 6–4.

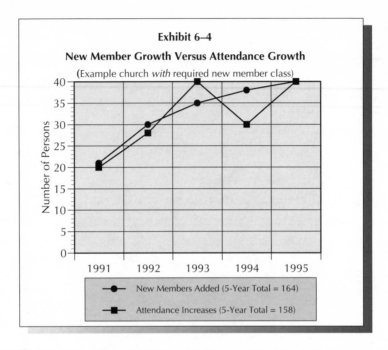

Exhibit 6–4

New Member Growth Versus Attendance Growth

(Example church *with* required new member class)

- ● New Members Added (5-Year Total = 164)
- ■ Attendance Increases (5-Year Total = 158)

When the church began the new member class, the number of membership additions declined dramatically. The twenty-one new members added in 1991 represented a fifteen-year low for the church. But the leadership did not panic. By 1992 annual additions were up to twenty-eight, still low from previous levels, but something noticeable was transpiring. Attendance was increasing at about the same pace as the number of new members. By 1993 the number of new members added was thirty-five, about the same number in the years when no membership class was required. Amazingly in 1993, attendance actually increased by more than the membership growth.

After five years, the church declared that their experiment had been a great success. Except for the first two years after the membership class had begun, membership additions were back to their healthy pace of thirty-five to forty per year. But attendance growth was nearly matching membership growth in the five-year period. And remember, in the previous five-year period, attendance growth was only one-third of membership growth.

Can we say dogmatically that a new member class will inevitably produce this same type of growth and high assimilation rate? The answer is no, but with explanations.

First, we did not have data on all the churches in the study for a ten-year period, as was the case in the example church shown in exhibits 6–3 and 6–4. Our lack of a large pool of data for a ten-year period would make our assessments inconclusive on this issue.

Second, it is impossible to isolate the new member class from other variables, such as pastoral leadership, theological leanings, preaching styles, and numerous other factors. Again, the best assessment we could have would be a statement of likelihood rather than causation.

Still, the limited data and anecdotal information is persuasive. So many church leaders shared with us similar experiences on initiating a new member class. They spoke of struggles to win its acceptance by church members. They shared with us initial declines in new member additions for a brief period of time, typically two years. And they rejoiced in dramatic turnarounds in retention rates. This pattern was repeated too many times to be ignored.

The Content of New Member Classes

If the evidence leads to the conclusion that a new member class does affect the retention rate in churches, then we must next ask what the contents of these classes include. This next section will describe briefly different topics in the classes.

Before the description of the classes is given, let us look at a summary of the different topics that we included. The topics are listed below in order of their frequency of use in the churches studied. The percentage indicates the proportion of the churches that include the topic in their new member classes.

Doctrine of the Church

More than any single topic, doctrine was considered the most critical issue to be covered in a new member class. A California pastor articulated the reason well: "I recently heard a preacher say, 'Our churches don't need doctrine, we just need Jesus.' Well, I confronted him after he preached, and

Exhibit 6–5
Topics Included in the New Member Class

1. Doctrine of the church (67.0%)

2. Polity/government of church (66.0%)

3. Examination of church constitution (64.6%)

4. Purpose of the Lord's Supper/Communion and baptism (63.5%)

5. Examination of church covenant/church discipline (63.2%)

6. Policies for church discipline/exclusion of members (62.5%)

7. Expectations of members after joining (58.7%)

8. History of church (56.5%)

9. Tour of church facilities (56.4%)

10. Denominational information (51.6%)

11. Plan of salvation (49.1%)

12. Tithing/financial support of the church (47.4%)

13. Method/meaning of baptism (41.1%)

14. Requirements for membership (38.9%)

15. Current opportunities for service in the church (37.2%)

16. Training in spiritual disciplines (35.2%)

17. Introduction to church staff and leadership (33.7%)

18. Explanation of the church's mission and/or vision (32.6%)

19. Inventory of spiritual gifts (29.5%)

20. Structure/support of missions (21.4%)

21. Training for witnessing/evangelism (18.6%)

I asked him how he could even know who Jesus is without the teachings of Scripture. And that's what doctrine is—what we believe about the Bible."

The pastor was responding to those who downplayed the importance of doctrine. His church, of course, was one of the churches that began a new member class with the doctrine of the church. "We save ourselves a lot of problems on the front end," he said, "by stating clearly what we believe. We may lose some people early, but that sure is better than the trouble people may cause later on."

Two out of three churches included doctrine in their new member classes. Most of those churches *began* the class with a discussion of the church's beliefs.

Polity/Government/Constitution/History

I combined the various topics above because they all tell the story of the church. They tell about the governing structure of the church. The topics inform as to the decision-making process in the church. And they articulate the documents that govern church life.

Perhaps one of the more interesting facets of this topic was the history of the church. At first glance, the subject of history might conjure images such as founding members, buildings constructed, or other less-than-exciting topics. But as we examined further the content of the historical session, we found more revealing information.

Many of the church leaders wanted to give more than a bland historical narrative. Instead they highlighted, with blunt honesty, significant moments in the histories of the churches. Some examples include:

- the founding vision of the church,
- reasons for significant declines or church splits,
- major evangelistic harvests, and
- theological trends in the church.

The impression we received as we listened to the historical topics covered was one of "full disclosure." The church leaders wanted the prospective members to understand, both negatively and positively, the past as well as the present realities of the church.

Purpose of the Lord's Supper/Communion and Baptism

Over 63 percent of the churches explained the significance of the Lord's Supper or Communion in their new member classes. Slightly over 41 percent explained the method and meaning of baptism. Baptism was more often discussed in a setting for new Christians only, so its discussion was not as prevalent in a class for all prospective members.

Examination of Church Covenant/Church Discipline

Many churches are using their church covenant with increasing frequency. This reflects the rising expectations of members of evangelistic churches.

It is therefore no surprise that the church covenant is often first examined in the membership class. Over 63 percent of the churches reported using church covenants in the class. A pastor in Kentucky, whose church requires adherence to their church covenant, explained that this discussion often reduces the number of prospective members. "When they hear what we expect of them," the pastor told us, "we lose quite a few. They tell us that they just can't be the kind of member we expect. But that's okay. I'd rather discover that at this stage than later on."

Covenantal relationships between church members and the church are sometimes called *formative discipline*.[2] We often think of church discipline as corrective action, even exclusion from membership. Such action is more properly called *corrective discipline*.

Formative discipline is concerned with establishing guidelines and expectations. It sets the parameters outside of which corrective discipline will take place. In simplest terms, formative discipline provides the rules, while corrective discipline is the punishment for breaking the rules.

The vast majority of churches in America today do not exercise church discipline. And yet moral failure is common among many members of evangelical churches. Even more common is the lack of commitment of other church members. Most evangelical churches accept *inactive members* as a normative term rather than as a theological oxymoron.

Though no single reason can explain the dearth of corrective discipline in our churches today, the failure to provide formative discipline seems to be at least a partial explanation. We are unable or unwilling to discipline members because we have not established clear expectations of what it means to be a part of God's church.

Expectations Stated/Requirements for Membership

By the time you have read this far in this book, you will have realized that the theme of this research has been expectations. Closely related to the issue of formative discipline is the articulation of expectations for members of the church.

A pastor in Georgia said: "In our new member class we tell the prospective members what we expect of them. We tell them about worship attendance, Sunday School attendance, stewardship, and other important matters. We don't tell them that they must do as we say, but we strongly encourage it."

Even more closely related to formative discipline are *requirements* that are mandated for membership. Relatively few of the churches actually mandated specific requirements to be a member. While nearly 6 out of 10 churches were willing to state expectations of members, only 38 percent mandated membership requirements.

The key to both the articulation of expectations and the clarifying of requirements is that both are done in the membership classes. These churches do not wait until the people have been members for several months before providing expectations of discipleship and ministry. The expectations or requirements are stated on the front end.

Tour of Church Facilities

Somewhat surprising was the number of churches that included a tour of the church facilities for the new or prospective members. Over 56 percent of the churches deemed the issue sufficiently important to take the new member class on a thorough visit of the church facilities.

This tour was done in over half of the churches in every size category. Even many of the smallest churches in our study provided tours. What were the key areas in the church building in which the prospective member had an interest? Younger families with children, we were told, inevitably asked to see the preschool or nursery facilities. Women of all ages asked for the different rest room locations. Men were interested in finding the easiest path to their Sunday School classes.

The church leaders told us that women frequently seemed more interested in the tour than men. An associate pastor told us, "Most men put up with the tour rather than enjoy it."

Denominational Information

For the writing of this book, our research team examined Southern Baptist churches only. But we now have information on more than two hundred churches that are not part of the Southern Baptist Convention. And, as in our previous study of effective evangelistic churches, we found little difference between the Southern Baptist churches and other churches. In fact, we found that evangelistic churches had more in common with each other than with churches in their own denominations.

When we state that slightly over half of the churches discuss their denominations in new member classes, we can say with a high level of confidence that we are referring to all churches; of course, independent and nondenominational churches would have no reason to discuss denominational issues.

In our postsurvey interviews, we heard from many church leaders who have just begun to include denominational information in their new member classes. It is indeed possible that, at least among the evangelistic churches we studied, churches are becoming more denominationally oriented.

Plan of Salvation

Nearly half of the churches gave a clear gospel message in their new member classes. A pastor in Florida spoke words that were repeated by other church leaders: "We don't assume that anyone is a Christian when they come to our [new member] class. We will share a message of salvation with everyone, including twenty-year Baptists. And we have seen several saved during the class."

Tithing/Financial Support

Slightly over 47 percent of the churches provided instruction on financial support in general and tithing in particular. These churches were bold about spelling out God's expectation of obedient stewardship for all Christians.

Opportunities for Service/Spiritual Gifts Inventories

A significant number of churches in our study used the new member class as an opportunity to offer places for the members to serve. Slightly over 37 percent either offered or required service opportunities. Three out of ten churches asked those in the new member class to complete a spiritual gifts inventory.

I am often asked if any particular spiritual gifts inventory was used more frequently than others. Though we did not inquire of every church in the study, fifty-three churches responded that they used sixteen different inventories. No particular inventory was dominant among those churches.

An important philosophy of the churches that present ministry opportunities in a new member class is that membership is contingent upon ministry. Members are expected (sometimes required) to be in a place of ministry, and service in the church is a requisite for membership.

Training in Spiritual Disciplines

The new member class is also a place where some churches introduce the members to spiritual disciplines. The most frequently mentioned disciplines were prayer and Bible study. Some churches taught prayer and fasting together as a spiritual discipline. Thirty-five percent of the churches in our study included these issues in the new member class.

Introduction to Church Staff and Leadership

A third of the churches in our study helped new members become familiar with staff or lay leadership in the church. More often than not, the persons introduced were physically present during these get-acquainted sessions.

Explanation of the Church's Vision and/or Mission

The vision and mission issue is a critical facet of effective assimilation (see chapter 8). Repeatedly we heard from church leaders the importance of spelling out the mission or vision of the church.

With so much emphasis placed on vision and mission by the church leaders, we were not surprised to see it included as an element of new member classes. Our surprise, however, was that only one-third of the churches in the study *did* include vision and mission issues in the new member classes.

The articulation and understanding of the mission of the church were key to a church's assimilation. I encourage you to study our research presented in chapter 8. It would appear that this issue is of such vital importance that it must be included in the "frontend" orientation of the new member class.

Structure and Support of Missions

In our previous study of effective evangelistic churches, we found a positive correlation between churches that support and do missions beyond their immediate community and the local churches' evangelistic success.[3] We discovered that the healthiest churches understood Acts 1:8, that is, to be a witness both in the surrounding area and to the ends of the earth.

We noticed in the study an increasing commitment of evangelistic churches to give to mission causes, to send mission teams around the world, and to create a world missions awareness and climate. Now over one out of five churches in our study discuss the missions issue before people become members of their churches. Based upon our two major research projects, watch for the missions issue to become even more discussed in years ahead.

Training for Witnessing and Evangelism

We typically think of witness training as something that takes place after a person has been a member for several months or even a few years. But in nearly one out of five of the churches, the leaders offered training before membership.

"We create a climate for evangelism," said a minister of education, "where we expect all of our members to be involved in personal evangelism. So we are introducing basic witness training before someone joins our church. It seems to have made a huge difference."

Who Teaches the New Member Class?

The pastor is the primary teacher in the new member class. Though his schedule is among the busiest, he sees this class as a primary opportunity to establish the vision and expectations, and to at least meet people before they join.

Who Attends the New Member Class?

Most of the people who attended new member classes in the churches in our study were either new members or applicants for membership. We found in the vast majority of churches, however, that visitors and prospects were either permitted or encouraged to join. Typically the prospects' attendance in the class did not commit them to membership. It did, however, provide them an opportunity to see the church from the inside, particularly when the pastor taught the class.

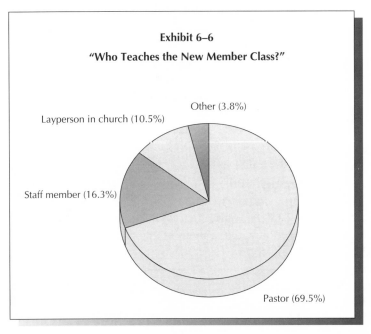

Exhibit 6–6
"Who Teaches the New Member Class?"

Other (3.8%)

Layperson in church (10.5%)

Staff member (16.3%)

Pastor (69.5%)

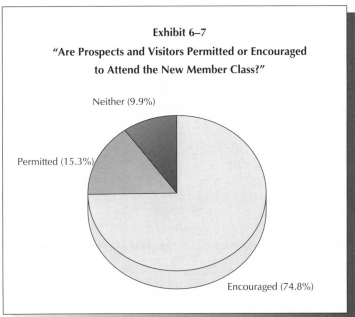

Exhibit 6–7
"Are Prospects and Visitors Permitted or Encouraged to Attend the New Member Class?"

Neither (9.9%)

Permitted (15.3%)

Encouraged (74.8%)

When/How Often Does the New Member Class Meet?

Another surprise regarding the new member class was its brevity. Nearly seven out of ten churches had a new member class that met for one day only, and that day was typically a Sunday.

An associate pastor explained this phenomenon: "We used to have new member classes over several weeks. But we had problems with continuity. Some people were out of town. Our restart time for fellowship and catching up others was a problem. So we ultimately decided to do our entire class in one six-hour session."

Our obvious question to the associate pastor concerned their church's ability to cover so much information in such a short time. He responded, "You're right, we can't go into much detail in one day. But we consider the class an introduction with the thought that deeper instruction, both formal and informal, will follow later."

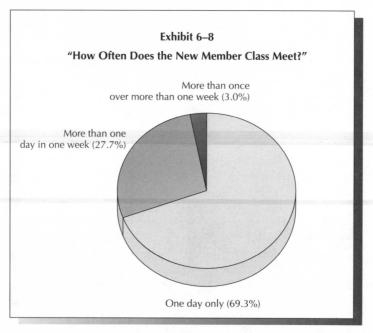

Exhibit 6–8

"How Often Does the New Member Class Meet?"

More than once over more than one week (3.0%)

More than one day in one week (27.7%)

One day only (69.3%)

Conclusion: Starting a New Member Class

The pastor in our survey had been with his church for over a decade. When he called my office, he was very anxious to know any results from this research. When I told him about the high positive correlation between required new member classes and assimilation, his silence spoke of his disappointment with the results.

"My church," he said carefully, "is located in a small, sleepy town in a very traditional area. We have been blessed with a number of souls saved in the past few years. But we still have the back-door problem."

He continued, "You said that new member classes have been very important in closing the back door, if they are required. You must understand that our church would never buy that. I've been there long enough to know that we can't require people to go through the class to be a member. What do we do?"

Fortunately, I do not have to depend upon my own wisdom to respond to the pastor. We interviewed a number of pastors who told us their stories. Basically, churches whose members resist the change to a required membership class have taken two steps to transition to this level.

Some churches take the first step by moving toward optional membership classes. Prospective members are not *required* to attend a membership class, but they are strongly encouraged to do so.

Admittedly, the optional class has less impact on the assimilation process than a required class. But this step can be a move toward higher expectations later.

A second stage that some churches have made is to require new members to attend the class, but not to require other members to do so. This process is often called "grandfathering" members and can be more palatable to existing members.

The key issue is that a new member class as a requisite entry point for membership in the church has a dramatic impact upon assimilation. Though only 18 percent of the churches in the study require such a class, those churches were among the most effective in closing the back door.

The data cannot be ignored. New member classes raise the level of expectations in churches. And higher expectations result in more effective assimilation. The move toward required membership classes will be one of the most interesting trends to observe in the years ahead.

CHAPTER 7

After They Join

Is there anything in the Bible about inactive church members?
Question asked by a Virginia pastor in our survey

Can you imagine Luke adding a sentence or two to his account of the early church in the Book of Acts? Perhaps the words would say, "And the Lord added to their number daily those who were being saved. But within two years, 60 percent of those saved were no longer active in the church."

The absurdity of such words reflects the absurd condition of the church in America today. While we would never believe that Luke would write these words, we often accept the fact that only 40 percent of our church members will be in attendance on a given Sunday. In fact, some church leaders brag about days when their attendance is 50 percent of their membership.

By this point in the book, I hope you have heard the clear message that assimilation is a process that begins *before* a person becomes a church member. Some writings on assimilation would lead you to believe that the process takes place completely after they join. While we cannot leave assimilation activity totally to the postjoining stage, neither can we ignore this stage and its importance in retention.

In this chapter as we look at the evangelistic churches in our study, we will attempt to discern what paths they take in assimilation after members join. We will look at the issue from three perspectives: new Christians, all members, and inactive members.

Assimilating the New Christian into the Church

In our research, we repeatedly heard anecdotal information about the critical importance of *immediately* assimilating new Christians into the church. Indeed, we were told by many church leaders that the first week after a person's profession of faith is the most critical time.

Exhibit 7–1
"After a *new convert* has made a profession of faith in your church, how quickly does follow-up activity take place?"*

Activity	N/A	Within 24 hrs.	Within 48 hrs.	Within 1 wk.	Within 1 mo.
Counseled by a decision counselor	1.0%	72.0%	15.0%	12.1%	0.9%
Provided a Bible	13.6	69.6	4.0	11.0	1.8
Given information explaining baptism	39.8	27.2	3.8	18.8	10.3
Assigned to a deacon or shepherd group	2.9	52.9	5.5	30.5	8.2
Contacted by a deacon or shepherd group leader	42.3	22.6	4.4	16.4	14.2
Assigned to a Bible study group or Sunday School class	40.3	9.2	3.7	25.6	21.2
Contacted by a Bible study group or Sunday School class leader	19.0	31.9	5.5	38.8	4.8
Assigned to a sponsor/ discipler	14.8	7.0	5.6	54.4	19.1
Contacted by a sponsor/ discipler	80.4	5.5	1.6	9.8	2.7
Contacted via a letter/phone call from church staff	77.4	1.6	2.7	13.6	4.7
Contacted via a visit from church staff	12.9	22.4	28.3	34.2	2.2
Provided offering envelopes	25.8	8.0	10.2	43.2	12.9
Provided a tour of church facility	30.3	9.7	3.0	25.8	31.1
Given a church directory	4.0	2.6	0.4	19.5	73.5
Given study material for new believers	66.7	4.0	11.3	5.0	13.1

*Note: N/A means the church does not use the follow-up activity.

Exhibit 7–1 reveals some rather amazing information. The high-expectation churches in our study respond very quickly after a person accepts Christ and makes his or her decision public. A pastor in Virginia explained: "We consider discipling the new Christian one of the most important things we do. And we believe that time is of the essence." He continued, "We found that, if we don't get to the new Christian quickly, he will probably not become involved in the church, and he will also remain a babe in Christ." '

Combining the three categories that include the period within less than one week reveals some interesting information. When we asked church leaders when they counsel new believers, 98.1 percent of the churches responded that this activity takes place within one week! (See exhibit 7–2.) Only 1 percent of the churches did not provide decision counseling at all.

In exhibit 7–3, we see that 89.0 percent of the churches assign a new believer to a deacon or shepherd group within one week. This activity indicates that the churches have a system for engendering accountability from the new Christian very quickly after his or her profession of faith.

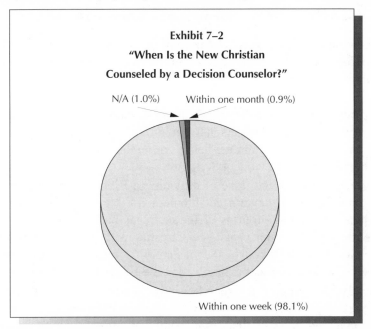

Exhibit 7–2
"When Is the New Christian
Counseled by a Decision Counselor?"

N/A (1.0%)   Within one month (0.9%)

Within one week (98.1%)

Another clear indication of the seriousness these churches place on assimilating new Christians was the quick response to get a Bible in the

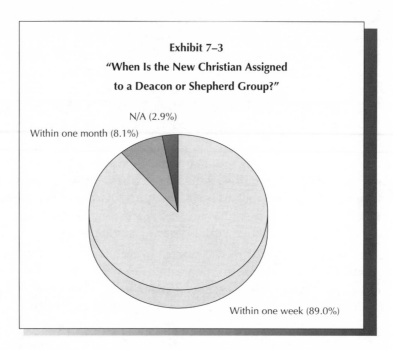

Exhibit 7–3

"When Is the New Christian Assigned to a Deacon or Shepherd Group?"

N/A (2.9%)

Within one month (8.1%)

Within one week (89.0%)

hands of new believers. Over 84 percent of the churches provide a Bible within one week, and nearly seven out of ten churches provided a Bible within twenty-four hours.

A minister of education in Arkansas expressed common sentiments about this issue: "We believe that the best way for a new Christian to mature in Christ is for that person to get into the Word." It is not surprising that almost all of these churches held a conservative theological viewpoint which included a high view of Scripture.

Closely related to the issue of providing a Bible was the widely held belief that the new believer needed to be in a Bible study class with other Christians. Over three-fourths of the churches had a Sunday School or Bible study leader contact each new Christian within a week of his or her profession of faith. Of course, the reason for the contact was to encourage the new Christian to become involved in the Bible class immediately.

Nearly 85 percent of the churches in our study sent a staff member to visit the new Christian within one week. Clearly, the overwhelming number of churches believed that discipleship was an issue calling for immediate response by the church. Indeed, the issue was deemed sufficiently important for one or more staff members to make an in-home visit.

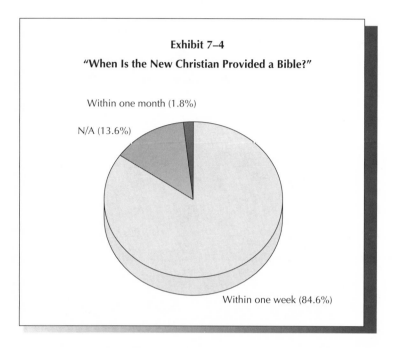

Exhibit 7–4

"When Is the New Christian Provided a Bible?"

Within one month (1.8%)

N/A (13.6%)

Within one week (84.6%)

The high-assimilation churches demonstrated several common characteristics in their attitudes or behaviors toward new Christians. Let us highlight some of these critical issues:

- The most common belief in assimilating new Christians was that immediate action by the church was imperative. The preceding graphs provide only a sample of the sense of urgency that prevailed in the churches.
- Another key issue was the establishment of relationships with the new believer. The most effective relationships toward assimilation were those formed with Christians *before* the new believer became a Christian.
- The vast majority of the churches (94.5 percent) believe that a new Christian should become involved in a place of service as quickly as possible. Of course, these churches restricted some ministries, such as teaching, to more mature believers.
- Almost all the churches attempted to get new Christians involved in both personal and class Bible study.

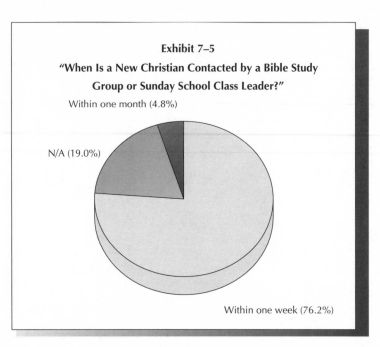

Exhibit 7–5

"When Is a New Christian Contacted by a Bible Study Group or Sunday School Class Leader?"

Within one month (4.8%)

N/A (19.0%)

Within one week (76.2%)

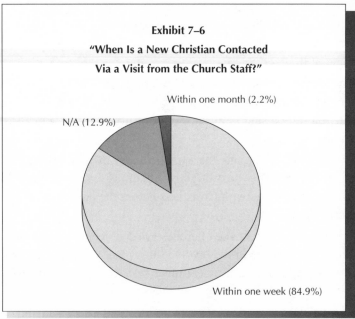

Exhibit 7–6

"When Is a New Christian Contacted Via a Visit from the Church Staff?"

Within one month (2.2%)

N/A (12.9%)

Within one week (84.9%)

- Financial stewardship issues were not postponed until the new believer progressed in spiritual maturity. Indeed, stewardship teachings and the providing of offering envelopes took place within one week of conversion in 61.4 percent of the churches.
- Most of the churches (71.2 percent) did not place age limitations on the baptism of children who had accepted Christ.
- Nearly six out of ten churches required the new believer to attend two different classes, one for new Christians and one for new members.

Finally, let us see the *primary influences* that the new Christian articulated in his or her acceptance of Christ. Two key issues were raised. One of these is commonly known, but the other may be a surprise.

The commonly held issue is that relationships are critical in bringing someone to Christ. In 48 percent of the conversions, the new Christian was introduced to Christ by a friend, family member, or coworker, who also invited him or her to church. Another 10.9 percent came to Christ through a special event or revival service, after being invited by a member.

If you combine the two types of invitations by church members, nearly 60 percent of the professions of faith came as a result of a church member's invitation. This data confirms numerous other studies and anecdotal information that assert the power of a simple invitation to church in leading someone to Christ.

Perhaps a more surprising aspect of the influences in leading someone to Christ was the role of Sunday School. First, 11.3 percent of those who came to Christ attended Sunday School class on their own and found Christ through Bible study and Christian fellowship. This influence is the third highest of any of the categories, and it is not much smaller than the 16.1 percent who came to a worship service on their own and found Christ.

Additionally, in our follow-up interviews, we found that half of the 48.0 percent who came to Christ after they had been invited to a church by a member entered first through Sunday School. *In other words, over 35 percent (11.3 percent + 24 percent) were significantly influenced by the Sunday School in their decision to accept Christ.*

This information is revealing if not astounding. Many pundits have assumed that the role of Sunday School in evangelism has all but disappeared. Our data indicate that the Sunday School had a role in over one out of three of those who accepted Christ!

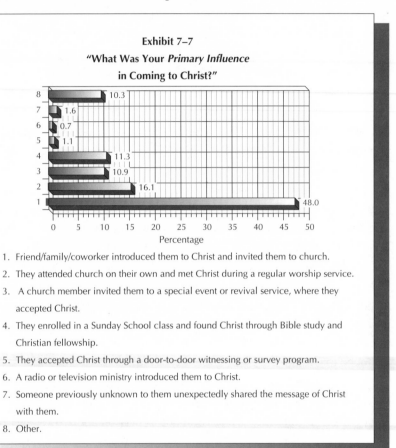

Exhibit 7–7

"What Was Your *Primary Influence* in Coming to Christ?"

1. Friend/family/coworker introduced them to Christ and invited them to church.
2. They attended church on their own and met Christ during a regular worship service.
3. A church member invited them to a special event or revival service, where they accepted Christ.
4. They enrolled in a Sunday School class and found Christ through Bible study and Christian fellowship.
5. They accepted Christ through a door-to-door witnessing or survey program.
6. A radio or television ministry introduced them to Christ.
7. Someone previously unknown to them unexpectedly shared the message of Christ with them.
8. Other.

The Assimilation of All Church Members

Sunday School is clearly the primary instrument by which churches in our study assimilate their members on an ongoing basis. As we demonstrated in chapter 2, the Sunday School provides accountability, opportunities for ministry, biblical instruction, and the establishment of relationships. All of these factors contribute positively to assimilation in the church.

Specific discipleship ministries and programs beyond Sunday School were rarely deemed effective by the churches. Exhibit 7–8 depicts the churches' concerns with their discipleship ministries.

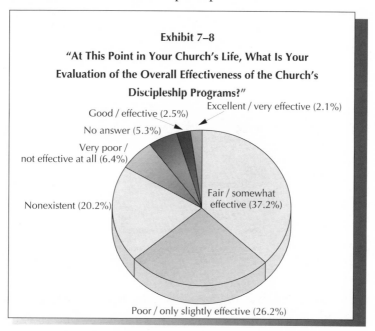

Exhibit 7–8

"At This Point in Your Church's Life, What Is Your Evaluation of the Overall Effectiveness of the Church's Discipleship Programs?"

Excellent / very effective (2.1%)
Good / effective (2.5%)
No answer (5.3%)
Very poor / not effective at all (6.4%)
Nonexistent (20.2%)
Fair / somewhat effective (37.2%)
Poor / only slightly effective (26.2%)

Though we have researched evangelistic churches, these churches are struggling with ideas and ministries to provide ongoing assimilation. The only approach that received widespread acceptance was assimilation through the Sunday School.

One assimilation process that we had expected to have significant acceptance was spiritual gifts discovery and utilization. After all, the discovery of spiritual gifts can help a believer find his or her place of ministry. And a person finding joy in a place of ministry is much more likely to remain actively involved in the church.

Our expectations were not met. Nearly six out of ten of the churches had no system or process in place to help people discover and utilize their spiritual gifts. "It's not that we don't want our members discovering and using their spiritual gifts," the California pastor told us. "It's just that we have yet to work out a system for keeping the process ongoing."

The higher-assimilation churches, however, were more likely to have some type of ongoing spiritual gifts program. They were not always satisfied with their process, but they viewed the issue as too important to do nothing. Exhibit 7–9 illustrates various sentiments in the different groups of churches.

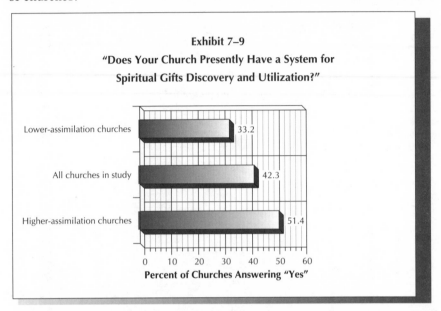

Exhibit 7–9

"Does Your Church Presently Have a System for Spiritual Gifts Discovery and Utilization?"

Lower-assimilation churches — 33.2

All churches in study — 42.3

Higher-assimilation churches — 51.4

Percent of Churches Answering "Yes"

Even fewer churches offered some type of one-to-one mentoring or discipleship ministry. Again, in our follow-up interviews, many church leaders told us that their Sunday School classes provided the ongoing discipleship emphasis, so they saw little need in creating yet another time-consuming program.

Overall, as shown in exhibit 7–10, only one-fourth of the churches offered one-to-one mentoring or discipleship programs. And these churches were no more effective at assimilation than the churches which did not offer one-to-one mentoring.

Conventional wisdom states that unmet needs are often stated as the reason people leave the church or become inactive. Though our research shows that this reason is not among the most significant reasons (further discussed in chapter 9), we were curious to see if the churches had a plan or plans to minister to the needs of all the members.

One issue pursued was the plan of personally "touching" every member of the church at least once a year. We did not define how each member was to be contacted. And the responses were varied. Those churches that did have an annual personal touch plan in place did so via letters, telephone

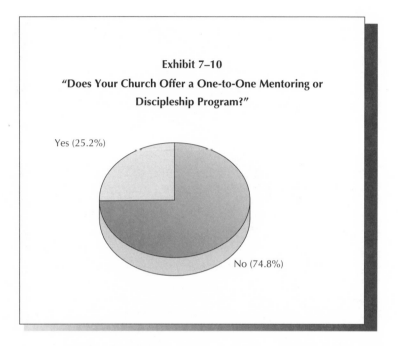

Exhibit 7–10

"Does Your Church Offer a One-to-One Mentoring or Discipleship Program?"

Yes (25.2%)

No (74.8%)

calls, deacon visits, Sunday School visits, and other means. Rarely did we hear that the pastor was the responsible party for contacting the members.

Four out of ten churches had a process where they contacted every member at least once a year. The most commonly mentioned responsible party for contacting the members was someone in the member's Sunday School class.

We also asked if the church had a specific process to assure that members requiring pastoral care were not overlooked. The pastoral care need could have been hospital visitation, ministering to those who are grieving, job loss, counseling, and others. This type of ministry was not uncommon. Nearly 64 percent of the churches had such a plan in place (exhibit 7–12).

Again, the primary ministering party was a person in the member's Sunday School class. Also, the higher-assimilation churches were much *less* likely to expect the pastor to do the bulk of pastoral care ministry than the lower-assimilation churches. Neither group of churches, however, perceived the pastor to be the primary caregiver to all members.

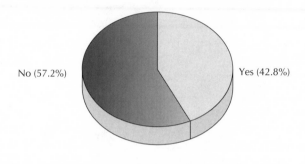

Exhibit 7–11

"Does Your Church Have a Plan by Which It Has an Individual Contact with Every Resident Member?"

No (57.2%)　　　　　Yes (42.8%)

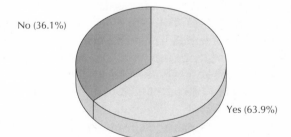

Exhibit 7–12

"Has Your Church Developed a Specific Process to Attempt to Assure that No Members Requiring Pastoral Care (Members in the Hospital, Deaths in the Family, Job Loss, etc.) Are Overlooked?"

No (36.1%)

Yes (63.9%)

Assimilating Inactive Members Back into the Church

Gathered around the table in the pastor's office were the five members of the ministry staff and me. The leaders of this North Carolina church were determined that membership was to have meaning in their church. For years they had experienced an average attendance of 40–45 percent of membership. This anemic rate was no longer acceptable.

The pastor spoke first: "As I see it, our numbers indicate that we have four distinct groups of members in our church: the very active, the fairly active, the nominally active, and the never present. Each group may require a different approach. Any suggestions?

The minister of education responded quickly: "I think we first must address the issue of the group that never attends. I don't think we have any business calling them members."

"Let's not move too fast," the associate pastor interjected. (His role was primarily pastoral care.) "Many of these members have been hurt deeply. And in many cases the church has been slow to respond. Sometimes we have been responsible for their pain. We can't just drop them from the rolls."

"So what do we do?" the youth minister asked. "Do we just keep them on our membership rolls and let them continue to pout?"

"Look," the music minister said, "not all of these inactive members were hurt by the church. I can think of six who used to be in the choir. They no longer attend church because they are no longer committed."

Sensing a lively debate was about to distract us from our purpose, I asked the ministerial staff to provide options for addressing the issue of inactive members. I told them to put any idea on the table, and we would address its merits later. Some of the ideas included:

- Visit all inactive members in their homes to try to determine why they are no longer active in the church.
- Drop from the rolls any member who has not attended church in the past year.
- Send inactive members a letter, asking if they would like to be removed from the rolls.
- Ignore the whole issue.
- Trade inactive member lists with a church in the city. Each church then uses the list as a prospect list.

The debate then proceeded and continued for two hours until a plan was devised. The plan included the following steps:

- Begin a three-month emphasis on the responsibility of membership. Send letters about this emphasis to every member.
- Announce a plan, to begin after the three-month emphasis, that deacons and other church leaders will be visiting the homes of members who have not attended church in the past six months.
- At the end of a twelve-month period, remove from membership anyone who has not attended in the past year.

I rarely go into a church where the issue of inactive members is not a major concern. As our research has shown, membership retention and activity are best addressed as a "frontend" issue, that is, expectations are stated clearly before a member joins.

Unfortunately, most churches have not dealt with membership expectations as a front-end issue. They consequently have a large number of members who rarely, if ever, attend. And the most common response has been to ignore the issue. But many churches today do not see avoidance as an option. Christ's church is just too important to treat with a cavalier attitude.

The churches in our study, though evangelistic and often desirous of high expectations, experienced many frustrations over inactive members. "The worst thing you can do," said a Colorado pastor, "is to get your staff and members to visit these people. Many of them are complaining, antagonistic, and self-centered whiners. I bet most of them need evangelistic attention instead of trying to reclaim them."

An Illinois pastor agreed: "I've stopped asking our members to visit inactive members. They just come back too discouraged."

In our study, we gave the churches five possible responses to the question: "What is your church's practice toward reclaiming inactive members?" The five options were:

- "Because our membership covenant requires attendance, we remove the members from our roll; we do, however, continue outreach/ministry toward that person."
- "We place inactive members on an inactive list, but we do not have a specific plan to reclaim them."
- "Inactive members are placed on an inactive list; we try to reclaim them with a specific plan."
- "Our church does not place members on an inactive list, nor do we have a plan for reclaiming inactive members."
- "Other."

Exhibit 7–13 shows the different responses. Note that only slightly over 5 percent of the churches have begun the process of removing inactive members from their rolls.

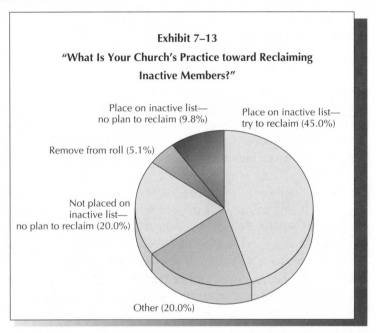

Exhibit 7–13

"What Is Your Church's Practice toward Reclaiming Inactive Members?"

Place on inactive list—no plan to reclaim (9.8%)

Place on inactive list—try to reclaim (45.0%)

Remove from roll (5.1%)

Not placed on inactive list—no plan to reclaim (20.0%)

Other (20.0%)

Though the highest number of churches are making some type of effort to reclaim inactive members, over one-third of the churches no longer have a concerted effort to do so. The Florida pastor expressed the views of many of the church leaders: "We could evangelize ten persons with the resources we use to try to reclaim one inactive member. As difficult as the decision may be, we have decided to send our people into fields that are white unto harvest."

Indeed, our research indicated that a twofold trend was taking place in churches in their attitudes toward inactive members. First, a few are exercising church discipline and removing them from the rolls. Second, a large group of churches has made the decision to reallocate resources away from inactive reclamation to prospect evangelization.

Ultimately, the churches are recognizing that "postjoining" assimilation efforts alone are ineffective. High expectations must be clearly articulated *before* a person joins the church. Only then will all the activities and ministries of discipleship and assimilation be most effective.

Conclusion

We found a few trends, if not a pattern, in our research of "postjoining" assimilation efforts. They can be seen in the following summary statements:

- Time is of the essence in any assimilation or discipleship efforts toward new Christians. Delays beyond even one week can be problematic.
- Bible study was deemed to be one of the best discipleship and assimilation approaches for new Christians. Both personal Bible study and involvement in Sunday School were critical.
- The primary influence (cited 48 percent of the time) in a person coming to Christ was an invitation to church by a friend, family member, or coworker.
- Sunday School was a "frontdoor" issue for the new Christians in over one-third of the cases studied. And when a person came to Christ through the Sunday School, he or she was much more likely to be assimilated.
- Churches that have a system for spiritual gifts discovery and utilization had a higher assimilation rate than other churches.
- Churches that have a plan for pastoral care to all members that does *not* depend on the pastor were more effective at assimilation than pastor-dependent churches.
- "Inactive members" is a theological oxymoron. The Bible never speaks of such a category of Christians. And churches have discovered that this group is one of the most difficult to reach.
- "Postjoining" assimilation activities alone are largely ineffective. The activities must be in partnership with "premembership" ministries and expectations. If churches wait until members have joined to begin the process of assimilation, they will most likely lose nearly half of them over the next five years.

So we return to the main discovery of our study. High-expectations are a key to assimilation. Postjoining activities of retention are helpful, indeed necessary. But they will be largely ineffective without clear expectations articulated before the person joins.

CHAPTER 8

Vision, Mission, and High Expectations

But one thing I do: forgetting what lies behind and reaching forward to what lies ahead, I press on toward the goal for the prize of the upward call of God in Christ Jesus.

The apostle Paul (Phil. 3:13–14)

We often stand amazed at the single-mindedness of the apostle Paul. In God's power, he accomplished so much in a relatively short period. Converted as an adult on the Damascus road, Paul made certain that every minute of his life was useful in the service of the Savior. He knew his mission, and his vision was clear.

As I speak with pastors around our nation, I hear from them that one of their great sources of frustration is their perceived inability to articulate a vision for their churches. An Ohio pastor expressed these sentiments: "I've read six or seven books about vision. And each of them has told me that if I don't have a vision for my church, then I'm a poor leader."

We asked that pastor what steps he had taken to discover God's vision for the church. He responded quickly: "I've done everything the books have said. I've prayed. I've researched our community and church. I have taken different tests and inventories to learn more about myself. Still nothing. Am I that dense? Am I that unusual?"

The answer to both questions is no. The pastor has experienced frustrations that are common to many church leaders. He desires to be the best leader God would have him to be, but he has great difficulty understanding God's specific plan for his church.

In this chapter we will present our findings in the areas of mission and vision. You may be surprised, as we were, at some of the results. First, we need to clarify the meaning of each of these words.

Understanding Mission and Vision

What is a mission statement? What is a vision statement? In a previous study we conducted, we observed considerable confusion over these phrases.[1] In this study we defined each of the terms. Our definitions may not be congruent with others, but at least those who responded understood clearly our meanings.

We first defined *mission*:

> *Mission—the primary purpose in which all Christian churches should be involved; these purposes typically include evangelism, discipleship, fellowship, ministry, and worship.*

We attempted to communicate in this definition that *all* churches should be involved in each aspect or purpose. By using our definition, churches should have similar mission statements.

The vision statement, however, is unique for each church:

> *Vision—God's specific plan for a specific church at a specific time*

Each church, therefore, would have a different vision statement unique to its own situation. It may have similarities with the vision statements of other churches but, ultimately, it would reflect the distinctive personality and community of each church.

Why do churches have vision statements or missions statements? In a perfect scenario, every church would accomplish God's purpose, and every church would accomplish that purpose with specifics according to its uniqueness. But the church today is not a perfect scenario. Indeed, church health seems to be deteriorating rapidly in our nation.

The mission and vision statements call the church back to its purposes. But the inference is that churches are not where they should be today. Some level of change, therefore, is needed to return a church to its basic mission.

The purpose of the mission and vision statement is thus to move the church from a less-than-desirable position to a more desirable position.

And such movement can only bring change. Typically, it is the change that the people resist (or their perception of what the change may look like), rather than the mission or vision statement.

Since the churches we studied were evangelistic churches, we expected them to be more responsive to change. As exhibit 8–1 depicts, our expectations were met.

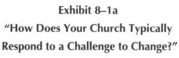

Exhibit 8–1a

"How Does Your Church Typically

Respond to a Challenge to Change?"

(Evangelistic Churches)

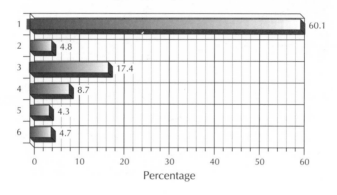

Percentage

1. Open to change as long as adequate study, prayer, and leadership support the change

2. Willing to change simply because the leadership suggests the change is necessary

3. Reluctant to change, but will do so when adequate study, prayer, and leadership support the need to change; change typically occurs slowly

4. Reluctant to change; changes grudgingly only when forced by circumstances

5. Usually unwilling to change, regardless of the issue

6. Other

If these exhibits accurately reflect the attitudes of the members of the churches, the evangelistic churches clearly are more receptive to change. Nearly two-thirds of the evangelistic churches were willing or open to change. In these churches, the adoption of new mission or vision statements will proceed on an easier path than in the nonevangelistic churches.

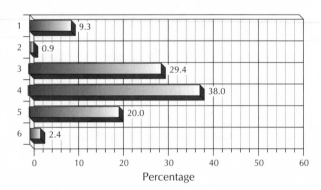

Exhibit 8–1b
"How Does Your Church Typically
Respond to a Challenge to Change?"
(Nonevangelistic Churches)

Percentage

1. Open to change as long as adequate study, prayer, and leadership support the change
2. Willing to change simply because the leadership suggests the change is necessary
3. Reluctant to change, but will do so when adequate study, prayer, and leadership
   support the need to change; change typically occurs slowly
4. Reluctant to change; changes grudgingly only when forced by circumstances
5. Usually unwilling to change, regardless of the issue
6. Other

Of course, our study did not determine causation. Were the evangelistic churches more open to change *because* they were evangelistic? Was change received more readily *because* their evangelistic efforts bring a constant flow of new persons into the church? Or were the churches more evangelistic because they were open to change? These questions remained unanswered in our study.

The Mission Statement Versus the Vision Statement

Our research team entered into this study fully expecting the more evangelistic churches to have precise vision statements. We were surprised to

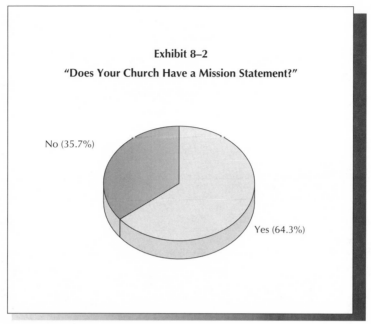

Exhibit 8–2

"Does Your Church Have a Mission Statement?"

No (35.7%)

Yes (64.3%)

find that the evangelistic churches were more likely to have mission state-ments instead of vision statements.

Exhibit 8–2 shows that nearly two-thirds of the churches have a mission statement. But exhibit 8–3 indicates that only four out of ten churches have a vision statement. What can explain the discrepancy?

A Kentucky pastor cogently explained why his church has a mission statement but not a vision statement: "The main thing our people need to learn is the purpose of the church. That never changes. But how we carry out the purpose, what [the survey] called vision, is always changing. It's dynamic. By the time our members could adopt a vision statement, God's vision for the church would probably have changed."

A key consideration to this aspect of the study is that the evangelistic churches were less likely to have vision *statements*. Such an observation does not mean, however, that the churches had no vision. It simply meant that the dynamic nature of God's vision for the church was such that it could not be captured in a document or statement that would have a long life.

Is there a relationship between conversion growth and the presence of a vision statement? Our work up to this point indicates that the higher the

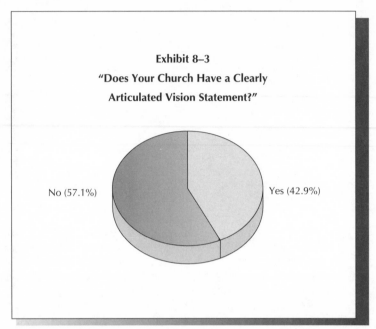

Exhibit 8–3
"Does Your Church Have a Clearly
Articulated Vision Statement?"

No (57.1%)   Yes (42.9%)

conversion rate of a church, the *less* likely the church will have a vision statement.

Let us see a sample mission statement and a sample vision statement so that the two can be compared and contrasted.

Sample mission statement:
Our church seeks to glorify God by reaching people for Christ, ministering to the needs of all, providing opportunities for people to grow in Christ, enjoying the fellowship of one another, and worshiping together.

In this mission statement all five purposes of the church are articulated. They are, in order of the mission statement above, evangelism, ministry, discipleship, fellowship, and worship.

Contrast the mission statement with this vision statement:

Sample vision statement:
Our church seeks to reach Baby Boomer parents and their children through ministries specifically geared to strengthen their families.

In this vision statement only two of the five purposes of the church are clearly evident, evangelism and ministry. But the evangelism has a specific target, the Baby Boomers. And ministry is geared specifically toward strengthening the families.

If the church with the vision statement above continues to target Boomers evangelistically, the ministry portion of the statement will change at the very least. Instead of family ministries, their twenty-first-century focus must be senior adult ministries!

The point is that the vision of the church is everchanging. And most evangelistic churches do not see the need or have the time to get the church to adopt a vision statement when it will likely change in the near future.

Understanding the Mission Statement

The question may seem absurd, but do you believe the church is more important than a hardware store? The reason I ask the question is because employees of a hardware store can likely tell you the different products that are sold in the store. They will show you the nuts, bolts, home-repair tools, and yard-maintenance items. They will take you down each aisle of the store and proudly point out hundreds of different products.

But ask a member of a church why the church exists. Ask someone to articulate the basic purposes of the church. In our follow-up interviews we asked hundreds of laypersons to name the purposes of a church. We did not give a limit on the number of responses they could give. Remember, the churches in this study are evangelistic churches, so the laypersons are exposed to evangelistic teachings, emphases, and messages on a regular basis.

We then asked the same question to a like number of laypersons from churches that did not meet our evangelistic criteria. We were looking for any responses that could be identified as the five purposes of the church we identified earlier: evangelism, discipleship, fellowship, ministry, and worship. A precise response was not necessary. For example, a response of "teaching the Bible" would be satisfactory for the discipleship purpose.

The results were amazing. Over 90 percent of the laypersons in the evangelistic churches were able to name at least four of the five purposes of the church. But only 17.7% of the laypersons in the nonevangelistic churches were able to identify four of the five purposes.

Let us grasp the gravity of this situation. Only 4 percent of the churches in America meet our evangelistic criteria. In 96 percent of our churches, therefore, the typical layperson cannot identify at least four of the purposes for which the church exists! This statistic is frightening. How can we

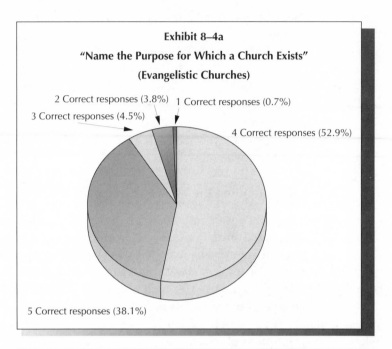

Exhibit 8–4a

"Name the Purpose for Which a Church Exists"

(Evangelistic Churches)

2 Correct responses (3.8%)   1 Correct responses (0.7%)

3 Correct responses (4.5%)

4 Correct responses (52.9%)

5 Correct responses (38.1%)

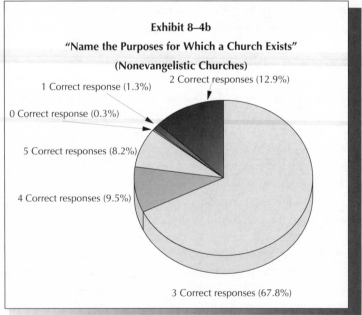

Exhibit 8–4b

"Name the Purposes for Which a Church Exists"

(Nonevangelistic Churches)

1 Correct response (1.3%)   2 Correct responses (12.9%)

0 Correct response (0.3%)

5 Correct responses (8.2%)

4 Correct responses (9.5%)

3 Correct responses (67.8%)

expect to have healthy churches when our members do not know why the church exists?

This next fact should not come as a surprise. The most frequently omitted purpose of the church was evangelism. This omission was particularly prevalent in the response of the laypersons in the nonevangelistic churches.

Now we can begin to see why understanding the mission of the church is so important. It is difficult, if not impossible, to motivate our members to be involved if they do not even know why the church exists. Such is the reason that the evangelistic churches in our study placed a high priority on communicating the mission of the church.

Exhibit 8–5 shows the importance of the mission statement in the churches in our study. Over 83 percent of the churches that had a mission statement considered it "very important" or "important" in the life of the congregation. Less than 3 percent viewed the mission statement as "not important."

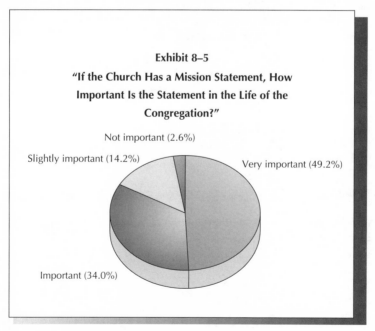

Exhibit 8–5
"If the Church Has a Mission Statement, How Important Is the Statement in the Life of the Congregation?"

Not important (2.6%)
Slightly important (14.2%)
Very important (49.2%)
Important (34.0%)

Because these churches saw the importance of their members understanding the mission or the purposes of the church, the leaders in the churches communicated them redundantly. An associate pastor in Florida explained, "Several years ago we were amazed to discover that many of our members did not have a clue as to why the church exists. So we began teaching the five basic purposes of the church."

The associate pastor found, however, that teaching the mission of the church is not a one-time event. He responded, "We soon learned that we could never stop teaching the mission. It's too important to forget. And the new members need to hear this message, too."

The churches communicate the five purposes of the church in a variety of ways. Exhibit 8–6 depicts the numerous means used to communicate the mission statement.

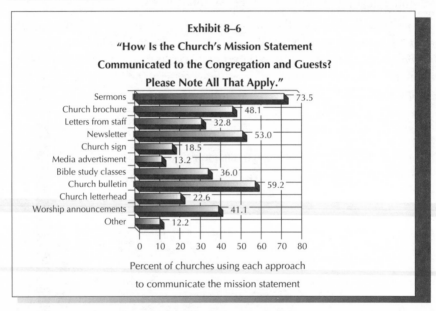

Exhibit 8–6
"How Is the Church's Mission Statement
Communicated to the Congregation and Guests?
Please Note All That Apply."

Approach	Percent
Sermons	73.5
Church brochure	48.1
Letters from staff	32.8
Newsletter	53.0
Church sign	18.5
Media advertisment	13.2
Bible study classes	36.0
Church bulletin	59.2
Church letterhead	22.6
Worship announcements	41.1
Other	12.2

Percent of churches using each approach
to communicate the mission statement

Why do these churches consider understanding the mission statement to be vital? In our follow-up interviews, the responses fell into seven categories.

The Mission Statement Explains Why the Church Exists

"Can you imagine being a part of any other organization," the Alabama pastor asked, "and not knowing why that organization exists? That's the problem we have in many of our churches today." As incredulous as it may seem, the vast majority of church members do *not* know the purposes of the church. Is it any wonder that they leave or become inactive? It is difficult to be involved in something you do not understand.

The Mission Statement Can Identify Deficiencies

I met with the leadership of a church in Mississippi. We wrote the five purposes of the church on a marker board. I asked them first to allocate the church budget into each of the purposes. Some of the items, such as personnel expenses, were difficult to estimate, but they made their best guesses.

We then looked at the allocation of time resources. If Sunday School, for example, involves eight hours of church calendar time each week, what proportion involves teaching, ministry, fellowship, or outreach?

The results were revealing. A very small portion of the church's budget and time was allocated to evangelism. This church's situation is not unusual. The mission statement helped the church to see where possible deficiencies existed.

The Mission Statement Can Keep the Church Balanced

It should not be the goal of every church to allocate an even 20 percent of resources to each of the five purposes. Some churches will have members with gifts that engender a more discipling environment; others may be more evangelistic. No church, however, should neglect any of the five purposes. Nor should any church allocate only negligible resources to one or more of the purposes.

The mission statement reminds the church that evangelism, discipleship, fellowship, ministry, and worship are all biblical functions of the church. Though a perfect balance between the five is rarely achieved, some level of balance is needed.

The Mission Statement Gives Reasons for Ministries in the Church

"When we evaluate all of our ministries each year," the pastor told us, "we always ask what purpose that ministry is accomplishing. Some are easy to discern," he told us, "but others are more difficult. Our food bank for example, is clearly a social ministry. But our Sunday School tends to meet four of the five purposes."

The pastor further explained that if a ministry or activity in the church does not meet one of the five purposes, they seek to adjust it or eliminate it. "The mission statement gives our ministries their reasons for existence. It keeps them focused as well," he said.

A Mission Statement Can Enhance Assimilation

The higher-assimilation churches in our study were more likely to have a mission statement than the lower-assimilation churches. While we cannot statistically prove that mission statements are a causative factor in higher assimilation, they do seem to have a positive effect.

"Church members want to be involved in something that has a clear purpose," the Texas pastor told us. "You can no longer expect people to be involved in church just because the pastor tells them to. But I also don't buy into the line that people won't give their time to the church. They'll give their time, money, and energy if it's something they believe in. You just have to let them know what the church is all about."

A Mission Statement Can Be an Evaluative Tool

Rick Warren likes to say that there are two basic questions for the church: "What's your business?" and "How's business?" The mission statement defines the "business" of the church. The statement is also a constant watch guard on all the church is doing. I recommend to church leaders that they evaluate their ministries each year, and ask "How's business?" for each of the five purposes.

The Five Purposes in the Mission Statement Are Biblical

Acts 2:42–47 provides a snapshot of the early Jerusalem church. It is our first picture of the new Christian church immediately following Pentecost. We sometimes call this passage "the model church" because it describes so clearly the five purposes of the church.

First we read that Christians were "continually devoting themselves to the apostles teaching" (2:42). The people were growing in Christ in *discipleship*. That same verse also says they devoted themselves to *"fellowship."*

In Acts 2:45 we find the Christians "began selling their property and possessions and were sharing them with all, as anyone might have need." The church was thus involved in *ministry*.

The early church quickly learned the importance of *worship*: "Day by day continuing with one mind in the temple" (2:46), they worshiped together. Then the author, Luke, tells us that "the Lord was adding to their number day by day those who were being saved" (2:47). *Evangelism* was at the heart of the early church.

Ultimately, the five purposes of the church are important because they are based on a biblical foundation. A church does not have the option of neglecting any of the five.

Understanding the Vision Statement

Only four out of ten churches in our study had a vision statement. The dynamic nature of God's vision for a church precluded many church leaders from putting the vision in writing. By the time the church would adopt the vision statement, God's specific plan for the specific church at a specific time would likely change.

Indeed, the better the assimilation rate of the church, the less likely the church will have a vision statement. The churches we studied are among the statistical elite of all churches in America. As we stated earlier, only 4 percent of churches would qualify for our evangelistic criteria. And then the higher-assimilation churches are the upper 50 percent retention churches among the evangelistic churches. They typically have dynamic ministries, programs, and leadership. So much is taking place that they cannot make a singular statement about God's plan for the church. If they are able to do so, something new often comes along by the time the church clearly articulates the vision.

While the churches are less likely to have a vision statement, they are still visionary. They may not articulate God's vision into a single, constant statement, but they know the importance of a clear idea and direction where God is leading the church. They do not often have vision statements, but they are constantly referring to a vision for the church.

In our follow-up interviews we asked the church leaders why a sense of God's vision is important in the lives of their churches. They gave us six major responses.

The Vision Tells the "How" of the Mission

The mission is applicable to all churches. It is a general statement of God's purpose for every church. The vision is a specific plan to carry out some aspect of the vision.

The mission, for example, calls for discipleship. Many churches in our study had very specific plans for helping Christians mature in their faith. They might utilize Bible study, one-on-one discipling, and specific discipleship programs. Their approach to discipleship might change from year to year.

The mission also calls for evangelism. Some of the churches had a specific evangelistic target. Others were successful at a broad-based evangelistic effort through the Sunday School. Still others had ongoing evangelism training for their members.

If the mission is the "what," the vision is the "how." And most of the churches in the study knew precisely how they were carrying out God's mission in their churches.

The Vision Helps a Church to Focus

There is no shortage of church growth and ministry ideas. Indeed, the barrage of books, conferences, and seminars can sometimes lead to confusion and overload.

Many of the leaders we interviewed understood their context and communities and the unique personalities of their churches. They knew that they could not try every new concept and program. The vision helped them to decide their specific focus, which eliminated many of the ideas and programs that other churches may be using.

The Vision Addresses the Uniqueness of Each Church

Every church has a unique personality. That personality reflects the member's gifts, passions, and strengths. A wise leader focuses the efforts of the church according to the uniqueness of the church. The vision articulates how the church's unique personality can best minister in its context and community.

The Vision Helps Allocate Resources

A church has limited resources of time, people, and money. Many churches today are busy with activities but with little sense of accomplishment. A Missouri pastor explained: "In the past, our people stayed busy at the church many hours every week. We were working hard, but we were frustrated because we saw few results." Three years ago the church tried a new approach. The pastor said, "Now we try to do fewer things better. We realize that we cannot do everything every other church does. Our resources are used to carry out our particular vision."

The Vision Engenders Accountability

Because the vision helps the church focus on doing fewer things well, greater attention can be given to the particular ministries outlined by the vision. When greater attention is given to individual ministries, a greater sense of accountability develops. "We are now much more aware of how well we are doing in certain areas," a Texas associate pastor told us. "When we used to try to do everything under the sun, we couldn't keep up. The quality suffered. Now we are much more accountable for what we do."

The Vision Fosters Cooperation Rather Than Competition

In many communities several churches are located in close proximity to one another. Some are even of the same denomination with virtually identical doctrinal beliefs. Why would a community need such similar churches?

If the churches understand God's specific plan for them at a specific time, each will have a focus that is unique and different from others. While there will undoubtedly be similar ministries offered, each of the churches can make unique contributions. The vision thus engenders a cooperative spirit rather than a competitive spirit.

An Encouraging Surprise

Our research team did not expect to find such a strong correlation between assimilation and a mission statement. Now that we have looked at the data and interviewed church leaders, the results make sense.

The vast majority of church members today do not understand the basic purposes of the church. How can we expect them to be involved if they do not understand what they are supposed to be doing? And how can we expect them to become assimilated into the life of the church until they are involved in ministries which they understand and to which they are dedicated?

The vision is also important, and we recently looked at six reasons behind its importance. But the mission must always precede the vision. Members must see the "big picture" before focusing on the details.

Why am I encouraged? I am encouraged because teaching the church its mission is simple and straightforward. It requires little change and rarely meets with opposition. Yes, such teaching requires work and persistence, but it is something any leader can do.

Helping the church understand its purposes may be the first step for many church leaders to close the back door more effectively. Nothing else can really be accomplished until church members realize why the church exists.

CHAPTER 9

Obstacles to Assimilation

As long as something does not change our wonderful church, I will support it.

From an interview with a church layperson in Mississippi

This book has attempted to demonstrate that churches will close the back door much more effectively when they have high expectations of their members. And these high expectations are understood clearly *before* someone joins the church.

Why, then, cannot every church in America become a high-expectation church? Why cannot most of the ideas we have learned from the churches in this study be implemented in every church? The answer is obvious. The move to become a high-expectation church requires significant change. And most churches in America are resistant to change.

At this point I want to refer again to two exhibits that were introduced in a previous chapter. Exhibits 9-1a and 9-1b show the attitudes of members in two groups of churches: evangelistic and nonevangelistic churches. Remember, by the criteria we established, only about 4 percent of the churches in America would be defined as evangelistic.

In evangelistic churches nearly 65 percent of the members are willing to change or they are open to change. But in the nonevangelistic churches only 10.2 percent of the churches are open to or willing to change. The discrepancy is huge!

Again, it is difficult to determine if an evangelistic attitude brings an openness to change or if an openness to change brings an evangelistic attitude. Our study cannot make dogmatic statements about causation. We *can* say, however, that evangelistic churches have fewer problems with change than nonevangelistic churches.

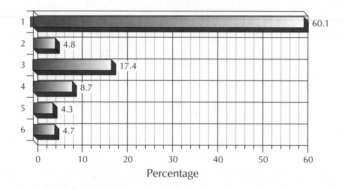

Exhibit 9–1a

"How Does Your Church Typically

Respond to a Challenge to Change?"

(Evangelistic Churches)

Percentage

1. Open to change as long as adequate study, prayer, and leadership support the change
2. Willing to change simply because the leadership suggests the change is necessary
3. Reluctant to change, but will do so when adequate study, prayer, and leadership
   support the need to change; change typically occurs slowly
4. Reluctant to change; changes grudgingly only when forced by circumstances
5. Usually unwilling to change, regardless of the issue
6. Other

Why Do They Leave?

At this point, we need to hear from the perspective of members who leave the church or become inactive. What are their reasons for leaving the church? Remember, we are asking for the perspective of inactive or former members of *evangelistic* churches. I would suspect that the answers would be significantly different if the questions were asked among nonevangelistic churches.

Exhibit 9-2 provides the somewhat surprising responses. We asked in the survey for the church leaders to give us the three most frequently cited

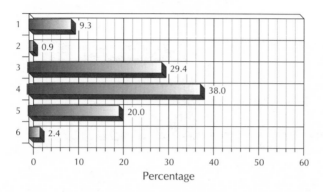

Exhibit 9–1b
"How Does Your Church Typically
Respond to a Challenge to Change?"
(Nonevangelistic Churches)

1. Open to change as long as adequate study, prayer, and leadership support the change
2. Willing to change simply because the leadership suggests the change is necessary
3. Reluctant to change, but will do so when adequate study, prayer, and leadership support the need to change; change typically occurs slowly
4. Reluctant to change; changes grudgingly only when forced by circumstances
5. Usually unwilling to change, regardless of the issue
6. Other

reasons members leave their churches. Of course, a better approach would have been to ask the former or inactive members directly. Our study, however, had to depend upon what the leaders of the churches told us. Other studies have dealt with interviews of the exiting members.[1]

Only four reasons were cited with any frequency by the respondents. Let us look at each of these four reasons.

Transfer of Job to Another Location

Over 70 percent of the respondents indicated that the primary reason members leave their churches is to transfer jobs to another location. In our

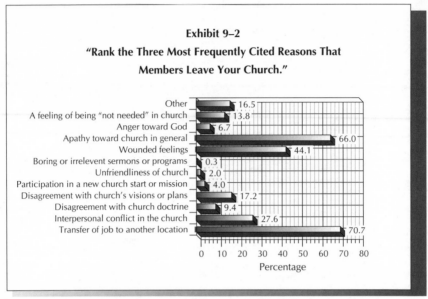

Exhibit 9–2

"Rank the Three Most Frequently Cited Reasons That Members Leave Your Church."

Reason	Percentage
Other	16.5
A feeling of being "not needed" in church	13.8
Anger toward God	6.7
Apathy toward church in general	66.0
Wounded feelings	44.1
Boring or irrelevent sermons or programs	0.3
Unfriendliness of church	2.0
Participation in a new church start or mission	4.0
Disagreement with church's visions or plans	17.2
Disagreement with church doctrine	9.4
Interpersonal conflict in the church	27.6
Transfer of job to another location	70.7

mobile society this factor is not unexpected. This issue, of course, is not an assimilation issue. In evangelistic churches, the first reason people leave is usually a positive reason. They have received a better occupational opportunity in another town or city. These departing members rarely leave unhappy.

Apathy toward Church in General

Nearly two-thirds of the respondents indicated that a major reason members leave or become inactive is nothing more than an apathetic attitude. Their excitement and enthusiasm for the church wanes. Other concerns in their lives take higher priority. They began to become less and less involved. Many times, when their final exit is made, their absences are hardly noticed.

How can someone be apathetic toward God's church? How can anything replace the priority of serving Christ through His church? As we attempted to understand this issue, we found three basic underlying responses.

"I'm not involved in anything." The most common reason for apathy was lack of involvement. The biblical metaphor, the body of Christ, makes it very clear that every member of the church is to be a functioning and

contributing part of the body. The New Testament church has no place for mere audiences or pew sitters.

When a member is not involved, who is to blame? Has the church failed the member, or has the member failed the church? Many times the answer is not immediately clear.

In some cases the church makes every opportunity for a member to become involved. From the first day he or she joins, deliberate and intentional efforts are made to get the new member serving in a place of ministry.

A few of the churches in our study addressed this issue directly. "We no longer vote to receive a new member until that person is involved in some type of ministry," a Florida pastor told us. "We believe that membership means ministry, and if people have a problem being involved, we don't think they're ready for membership."

The majority of church leaders, however, do not believe their churches are ready to mandate ministry involvement as a requisite for membership. Their approaches are encouragement and persuasion to the new members to become involved.

Though most of the evangelistic churches in our study have open and encouraging paths for members to become involved in ministry, a few church leaders admitted that involvement is difficult in their churches. "Sometimes I feel like our members make new people 'pay their dues' before they will let them do anything," a North Carolina pastor wrote. Many of our newer members eventually give up and move to a church where they can get involved. Some just drop out altogether."

Involvement is critical in the assimilation process. In our previous study of evangelistic churches, we found that ministry involvement, high expectations, and relationship building were the three critical keys to retention.[2] Our present research indicates that *lack* of involvement is one of the major reasons members drop out of active church life.

"I'm not getting fed at the church." A commonly stated reason for inactivity or withdrawal from the church is a sense that the member is receiving little from the church. These dropouts tell the church leadership that there are few opportunities for spiritual growth. They complain that the preaching is weak or that the Sunday School lessons are shallow.

We often disregard such complaints as spiritual immaturity—Christian whiners who expect to be served rather than to serve. After all, no one should have to depend upon others for spiritual growth. Indeed, when I was a pastor, I often felt that the exiting of such complainers was a blessed departure.

While such self-serving attitudes are likely signs of spiritual immaturity, perhaps they should not be disregarded altogether. If our research of the past several years has uncovered any significant negative trends, one of them would have to be a disturbing move toward more shallow preaching and less challenging Bible teaching. Perhaps we need to listen a bit more carefully to the critics, even if their spiritual maturity level is low.

"I have no friends at church." The development of relationships is crucial in assimilation. Many effective church leaders realize this issue, and they try several approaches to address it.

Several churches in our study assigned longer-term members to befriend new members. One church, for example, called the ministry "adopt a member." The church made every effort to match people with similar backgrounds such as age, family, and socioeconomic factors.

These types of ministries had limited success. Despite the best efforts of the church leadership, relationship matchmaking is rarely successful.

A more common approach, used by a majority of churches in our study, is to assign the new member to a Sunday School class. Of course, some of the new members were already in Sunday School classes before they joined the church.

This approach has proved more successful in developing relationships because the new member has more than one option. A Sunday School class by definition includes a few or several members. The new members thus have several people with whom they can develop relationships.

Many of the churches in our study were very aggressive in this approach. Some would not grant membership in the church until the prospective member had made a decision about membership in a particular Sunday School class. Other churches assigned new members to Sunday School classes, but they had no requirements for any level of involvement.

The most successful relationship-building strategy depended upon relationships built *before* the prospective member ever visited the church. An example from a church in Florida will illustrate best this approach.

Because the Florida church had such a high conversion rate *and* assimilation rate, I made the decision to visit the church over a three-day period. On Friday I interviewed the pastor, who shared with me the Sunday School records. The summary statistics were unlike any I had seen in other churches. Statistics were kept on each Sunday School class in four basic categories:

- enrollment—at the date of the report;
- attendance—twelve-month rolling average;
- number of baptisms—the number of people reached for Christ through the specific Sunday School class. The number of baptisms were for the past twelve months; and
- number of new classes—the number of new classes started by the specific Sunday School class. The period covered was the past eighteen months.

These one-page summary records were given to every youth and adult Sunday School class member every week. The church had an amazing "rewards" system that recognized evangelistic Sunday School classes, and classes with a "mission mind-set" to reproduce themselves.

Of particular interest to me was a Sunday School class that counted fourteen baptisms in the past twelve months and, amazingly, had started three new Sunday School classes in the past eighteen months. I decided to visit the class two days later. The pastor would later inform me that this same class had a retention rate of nearly 100 percent, excluding members who had moved out of town.

I arrived at the class at 9:00 A.M. on Sunday morning, fifteen minutes before the 9:15 A.M. start time. Much to my surprise, almost all of those who would be in attendance were already present, at least fifteen minutes before the class began. I would learn later that the teacher began the class promptly at 9:15 A.M., regardless of the number present. Any fellowship time had to precede the designated starting time of the class.

Most of those in attendance came with a Bible and a well-worn Sunday School lesson book. It was obvious to me that many, if not most, of the members prepared and studied their lessons each week. Visitors were given copies of the lesson upon their arrival.

What does all of this information have to do with assimilation through the building of relationships? I received the answer to that question when the class began promptly at 9:15 A.M. The teacher started with prayer requests in an unusual manner. The teacher first spoke to "Judy" and asked her how we might pray for "Betty." I would soon learn that Betty was a coworker of Judy's, and that Betty was not a Christian.

This pattern of prayer requests continued for ten or twelve class members, although each request was brief. The entire prayer time was less than ten minutes.

The pattern and strategy soon became obvious to me. Each member of the Sunday School class was expected to develop a relationship with a lost person. The prayer time was a low-key approach to accountability. The class was reaching numerous persons for Christ each year through relationship building in a Sunday School class.

I was curious. After the class I asked the teacher if any lost persons were present in Sunday School class. The response was a surprise introduction to two ladies who had attended the class. Neither of the women had yet accepted Christ.

I asked each of them what prompted them to start attending the class. One of the ladies tearfully told me of her recent divorce. She explained how her coworker, "Ann," a member of the Sunday School class, had been her friend during the entire ordeal. She attended Sunday School because of Ann.

The other lady pointed to "Debbie," a faithful member of the class. The lady's husband had lost his job, but her neighbor Debbie and Debbie's husband had stood by the couple in difficult times. They contacted several prospective employers for her husband, one of whom eventually made a job offer. The lady attended Sunday School because of Debbie.

I could now understand both the evangelistic effectiveness and the assimilation effectiveness of this Sunday School class and of the entire Florida church. Evangelistic accountability resulted in numerous decisions for Christ. This outreach approach was used for Christians looking for a church home as well.

Assimilation was so effective in the church because most relationships developed *before* a prospect ever visited the church. No special program was needed to foster relationship building. It is little wonder that this church had one of the best assimilation rates of all the churches we have studied.

Interpersonal Conflict/Wounded Feelings

The third and fourth reasons for member dropout were interpersonal conflict (cited by 27.6 percent of the respondents) and wounded feelings (44.1 percent). In any setting of several people, conflict and hurt feelings are inevitable. Yet some people leave in the midst of conflict, while others decide to remain. What determines their responses?

More than any other reason, the church leaders told us that the members who were more involved were less likely to leave in the presence of conflict or wounded feelings. Because more involved members had a greater investment in the church in their time, energy, and money, they were hesitant to leave at the slightest hint of problems. The issue of involvement thus returned to the forefront in assimilation.

Other Reasons for Leaving

After the four primary reasons cited above, the other issues, by numerical response, are minor. Only a brief comment will thus be made about each of them.

- Disagreement with church doctrine (9.4 percent). This issue seems to get more attention than it warrants. Less than one out of ten people leave over doctrinal matters.
- Disagreement with church's visions and plans (17.2 percent). Anecdotally we heard that this issue seems to arise more during a building program. Perhaps the members fear the anticipated requests for money!
- Participation in a new church start or mission (4.0 percent). This reason for leaving is healthy. We wish this number was higher!
- Unfriendliness of church (2.0 percent). We were somewhat surprised at the low number of responses to this reason.
- Boring or irrelevant sermons or programs (0.3 percent). Again, we were surprised. Less than 1 percent of the respondents found fault with the sermons or programs.
- Anger toward God (6.7 percent). A relatively small number of respondents gave this issue as a reason for departure.
- A feeling of being "not needed" in the church (13.8 percent). This issue overlapped with the issue of apathy, which had a higher response rate (66.0 percent).
- Other (16.5 percent). Over forty other responses were given.

In this first half of the chapter, we have looked at the perspective of the members who leave churches or become inactive. Many obstacles to assimilation, however, are inherent in the attitudes of church members. To that issue we now turn.

Obstacles in Attitudes

When we asked questions about the churches' vision and mission, we quickly learned that obstacles to change were ever present. Those obstacles were expressed in a variety of ways.

Realizing that the churches we studied were evangelistic churches, we compared their responses with over two hundred nonevangelistic churches. The contrasts were revealing.

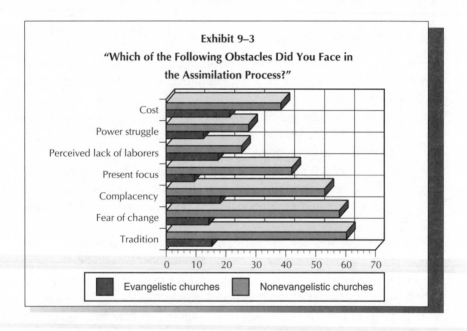

Exhibit 9–3
"Which of the Following Obstacles Did You Face in the Assimilation Process?"

Tradition: "We've never done it that way before."

Six out of ten of the nonevangelistic churches had problems trying to do things differently. Only 15 percent of the evangelistic church leaders considered this issue an obstacle.

Effective assimilation often requires a new paradigm. A required new member class, for example, can be a major departure from "the way we've always done it." Those churches that are the most effective in assimilation are churches that are willing to let go of tradition, when necessary, to make a difference for the kingdom of God.

Fear of Change: "How will our church and its programs change?"

Over 57 percent of the nonevangelistic churches indicated that change itself was a major obstacle to becoming a high-expectation church that assimilates effectively. "My church members see our church as the rock of stability in a world that has no stability," an Iowa pastor told us. His church was not included in our initial study because it did not meet the evangelistic criteria we established.

Although only 14.3 percent of the evangelistic churches indicated that fear of change presented a major obstacle to assimilation, they still affirmed that change was not always easy. "We made several changes in our membership requirements," a layman from Alabama told us. "It was not always easy," he said, "because we're used to doing things the same old way."

What made them willing to change? The layman responded: "We realized that we were not effective in our old paradigm. And we further realized that we had to make a choice between effectiveness for the kingdom and our own comfort. We decided to get out of our comfort zone."

Complacency: "We're happy the way we are."

Closely related to the change issue is the issue of complacency. Over half of the nonevangelistic churches were happy with their present state and had no inclination to change. Only 18 percent of the evangelistic churches indicated any problem with this attitude.

Present Focus: "We've got too many needs right now to begin thinking about what God wants us to do beyond today."

Forty-two percent of the nonevangelistic churches indicated that a lack of focus on the future was a major problem with assimilation. The attitude that was present essentially limited God. Many of the members could not conceive of new ministries and strategies because all of the present members' needs were not being met.

The contrast was stark with the evangelistic churches. Only 9.4 percent of the evangelistic churches indicated any kind of problems with a future focus. The vast majority of members in these churches believed in a God who was sufficient to meet present needs and to provide for new opportunities in the future.

Perceived Lack of Laborers: "Where will we get the workers to accomplish these tasks?"

About 25 percent of the nonevangelistic churches and 17 percent of the evangelistic churches saw a lack of laborers as an obstacle to assimilation. The percentage difference between the two groups of churches was smallest on this issue. The attitude is reflected in the comments of a woman from a church in Oklahoma, who said: "We don't have enough workers to fill all of our present positions. We sure can't do anything else until we've met this need."

Power Struggles: "Will I lose my position or authority in the church?"

When new approaches to assimilation are implemented, new emphases, programs, and ministries develop. The new arrangement of opportunities can change the leadership needs in the church. Sometimes those who feel they are in power are threatened by the new arrangement or prospective arrangement. This issue was perceived to be an obstacle in 27.6 percent of the nonevangelistic churches and in only 12.5 percent of the evangelistic churches.

Cost: "How will we pay for everything our new vision demands?"

In every church, leaders meet critics who think that any new idea is too costly financially. A rather high 38.4 percent of the nonevangelistic churches indicated that this issue was an obstacle to assimilation. It was not an unimportant issue in the evangelistic churches either. Over one in five of these churches indicated that objections to cost presented obstacles to effective assimilation.

How Effective Is Your Church?

Despite the possible obstacles to assimilation, the evangelistic churches in our study felt their overall effectiveness in assimilation was healthy. Over nine out of ten of the churches rated their assimilation effectiveness "fair" or "good" (see exhibit 9–4).

Yet most of the churches saw significant room for improvement. Only 3.2 percent of the churches were evaluated by their church leaders as "excellent/very effective."

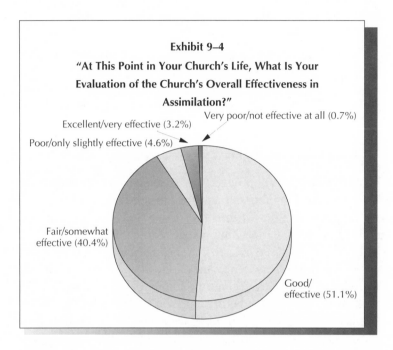

Exhibit 9–4

"At This Point in Your Church's Life, What Is Your Evaluation of the Church's Overall Effectiveness in Assimilation?"

Very poor/not effective at all (0.7%)

Excellent/very effective (3.2%)

Poor/only slightly effective (4.6%)

Fair/somewhat effective (40.4%)

Good/ effective (51.1%)

At the conclusion of our survey, we asked the church leaders the following question: "Now that you have completed this survey, what findings have surprised you about your church's assimilation process?" Listen to some of the following quotes. You will see quickly that these leaders see much room for improvement.

- "We are not doing a very good job of [assimilation]. We are certainly not doing much in an 'intentional' manner."
- "We need additional staff desperately!"
- "We've got a long way to go."
- "We could use a lot of work in this area."
- "Our [assimilation] process is weak and undefined. We have nothing written to follow."
- "We need more attention to detail in this area."
- "Before this survey, we hadn't thought of assimilation very much."
- "We need better programs that would fit our specific [assimilation] needs."

- "We need (1) more budgeting; (2) a more cohesive approach; and (3) probably a mentor for every new convert."
- "We do very little."
- "I'm amazed that we're still growing, not doing any more than we are. We need to be more intentional in our assimilation."
- "So much depends upon the leadership of the pastor, and so much depends on basic interpersonal relationships and friendship building."
- "Oh, well."

Concluding Thoughts: Obstacles and Opportunities

Obstacles to assimilation have two basic sources: the attitudes of the members who are dropping out and the attitudes of the church members who fail to assimilate new members. As our study has shown, rarely are programs or ineffective preaching reasons for leaving.

Another recurrent issue is expectations, particularly clearly articulated expectations *before* a person becomes a member of the church. Many of the assimilation obstacles became problems because churches failed to deal with issues early, if not before a person joined a church.

I recently met with the pastor of a 500-attendance church in a southern state. The church added 75 to 100 new members each year, but attendance had remained virtually the same for over 10 years. In other words, the church has an assimilation problem.

In my consultation with the church, I was able to share some of the results of this study. The pastor listened attentively. He acknowledged that many of the attitudinal obstacles to become a high-expectation church were present in his church.

He then asked a series of thought-provoking questions. How does he address attitudes that create obstacles? How can he become a more effective leader? And how can he implement some of the ideas that you the reader have learned in the previous chapters?

Good questions! Indeed, the questions led me back to the leaders who served high-expectation and effective-assimilation churches. How did you do it? How did you implement all the ideas that are so effective today? Their answers are in the next and final chapter.

CHAPTER 10

Lessons from the
High-Expectation Church

Many people are not moving with God today simply because they were not willing to take the small steps He placed before them.

John L. Mason

Over two thousand church leaders. Multiple voices of expertise from every region of the country and every size church. Enthusiastic leaders. Frustrated leaders. Joyous leaders. Broken leaders. Over the past several years, the research team of the Billy Graham School of Southern Seminary and I have had the opportunity to listen to leaders of evangelistic and high-assimilation churches.

In this book I have attempted to provide statistical data and interview information on the ministries, programs, and characteristics of churches that reach and retain people. In other words, I have explained more of the *what* than the *how*.

We took a significant portion of our interview process to try to understand *how* a leader moved a church from one point to another. In this final chapter, I will share with you their responses.

Fourteen Lessons from 287 Churches

The churches we studied are reaching significant numbers of people for Christ. Many are doing a good job of retaining the new members. But not all of these churches are located in high-demographic growth areas. And not all the leaders are "superstar" leaders. Many are quiet and unassuming. How then did these pastors and other leaders provide the leadership to make their churches high-expectation churches? We learned fourteen important lessons.

Lesson # 1: A Few Churches Have Unique Leaders

I think if I had gone to Orange County, California, in 1980 to plant a church, I would have seen a great demographic opportunity. Perhaps I would have targeted Saddleback Valley for my church, the fastest-growing area of Orange County, which was the fastest-growing county in the United States.

I have had the opportunity to lead four churches to growth in my own ministry. The results have been gratifying, and I might have seen some pretty good growth if I had started that church in 1980 in Saddleback Valley. But I seriously doubt that the church I started would have been anything like Saddleback Valley Community Church. I doubt that the church growth of my effort would have been close to the remarkable growth of the church started by Rick Warren.[1]

I see Rick Warren as a person with unique leadership skills. Other men like Adrian Rogers, Jerry Vines, James Merritt, Ed Young, and Buddy Gray—to name a few—are persons with leadership gifts that cannot be replicated. As we interviewed pastors of the churches in this study, we noticed several with certain leadership skills that could only be described as extraordinary.

It is erroneous to think, however, that only a few unique leaders can lead churches to be exciting and evangelistic churches. Other pastors have different leadership styles that can still make a difference. To that issue we now turn.

Lesson # 2: Most Successful Leaders Have Learned to Eat Elephants

Al Jackson is the pastor of Lakeview Baptist Church in Auburn, Alabama. In the nearly twenty years he has served the church as pastor, attendance has increased from two hundred to twelve hundred.

When you meet Al Jackson for the first time, you are not overwhelmed by a loquacious person with a gregarious personality. But you are soon impressed with his commitment and his love for people. You learn that this pastor has been willing to take small steps forward in the leadership of Lakeview.

Auburn is not a large and growing town. The community is dominated by Auburn University, but churches in college towns often struggle. College students are often the most difficult to reach. But at Lakeview, the college ministry is thriving and growing.

Al Jackson has patiently mentored men, a few at a time, in discipleship and ministry. Many of these men today are pastors, missionaries, and seminary students. The process has been slow and methodical, but the long-term results have been extremely gratifying.

Pastor Jackson has learned to "eat an elephant." How do you eat an elephant? One bite at a time. You are willing to make incremental gains which result in long-term blessings. Al Jackson has been through some painful years at Lakeview. From the inside, the growth and progress undoubtedly seemed slow. But he has been faithful. Today Lakeview is one of the strongest churches in our nation from almost any perspective.[2]

The vast majority of the pastors in our study testified to the often slow and even painful process of "hanging in there." Many shared the following stages of their pastoral tenure:

- honeymoon
- trial and testing, and
- renewed ministry and growth.

The third stage, renewed ministry and growth, sometimes did not take place until seven years or more had passed. But with average pastoral tenure just slightly over two years, only a few pastors ever see this stage.

The pastors were candid in their assessment of past mistakes. Some of the men indicated that they left other churches too soon. The typical reasons included the desire to escape conflict or an opportunity to move to a larger church. "I thought I could leave all my problems by leaving the church," a pastor told us. "When the opportunity came to go to a larger church, I jumped at it. Now I wonder if I should have stayed at the church and tried to deal with the issues. I've discovered that my present church presents some of those same problems."

We interviewed many pastors of long tenure. Though they would certainly indicate their willingness to move if God clearly spoke, they are determined to have a long-term perspective at their churches. Sometimes the progress seems snail paced, but they persistently attempted to move the church forward.

Some of the pastors indicated that one danger they face is becoming too comfortable. Leadership demands persistence and moving people out of their own comfort zones. But that type of leadership can engender conflict. "Sometimes it is just so easy not to rock the boat," another pastor told us. "I have to make certain I'm challenging the people, even when they feel like everything is just fine."

Lesson # 3: Move to Become a High-Expectation Church on an Incremental Basis

One very clear theme of our research was that high-assimilation churches are likely to be high-expectation churches. But rarely did we find a church that had transitioned to a high-expectation mode quickly. Church members are willing to make changes with three provisions. First, they must be informed; second, they must have time to think about it and to pray over it; and third, they must be certain that the leadership of the church is one spirit and one voice concerning the change.

A review of the data in exhibit 10–1 shows the predominant attitude of church members toward change. This attitude was particularly noticeable when dealing with issues of transitioning to become a high-expectation church.

Nearly nine out of ten of the churches will make changes, either eagerly or reluctantly, as long as study, prayer, and leadership unanimity are evident. Such a process takes time. For some of the churches, the transition to become a high-expectation church took ten or more years.

Lesson # 4: Intentionality Is a Big Issue

In our previous study of evangelistic churches,[3] we discovered the importance of intentionality in reaching people for Christ. The issue is no less important in assimilation. Some church leaders today expect something to happen because it should happen. Or they wonder why the laity are not doing their job.

When assimilation takes place in a church, the pastor, staff, and other leaders are working fervently to close the back door. They are persistent in their efforts. While they may get frustrated, they do not give up easily. Effective assimilation requires hard work, and the leaders must be visibly at the forefront of the efforts.

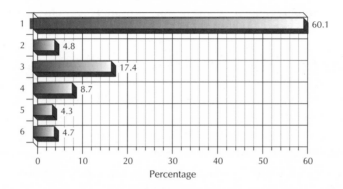

Exhibit 10–1
"How Does Your Church Typically Respond to a
Challenge to Change?"

1. Open to change as long as adequate study, prayer, and leadership support the change
2. Willing to change simply because leadership suggests the change is necessary
3. Reluctant to change, but will do so when adequate study, prayer, and leadership
   support the need to change; change typically occurs slowly
4. Reluctant to change; changes grudgingly only when forced by circumstances
5. Usually unwilling to change, regardless of the issue
6. Other

Lesson # 5: Sunday School Must Not Be Ignored

To say that Sunday School is important in effective assimilation would be redundant at this point in the book, but it would not be an overstatement. No programmatic methodology was deemed as effective at closing the back door as a quality Sunday School.

We observed that the effective Sunday Schools had strong and vocal support from the pastor. Indeed it was often the pastor who spoke most often about the importance of Sunday School. He did not leave the emphasis in the hands of a minister of education or a Sunday School director alone. The pastor typically was actively involved in training, recruiting, and promotion in Sunday School.

Annual Sunday School appreciation banquets were common in the churches with effective Sunday Schools. The pastor, because he realized its importance, would usually offer words of gratitude and encouragement to Sunday School workers at this banquet. But in churches where Sunday School was benignly ignored by the pastor, its effectiveness in assimilation was dramatically reduced.

Lesson # 6: A New Member Class Raises Expectation Levels

The majority of the churches in our study had a new member class. The classes existed at four basic levels:

- *Available*. The class is available for new or prospective members. No particular emphasis to attend is given.
- *Encouraged*. The class is not required, but new or prospective members are strongly encouraged to participate.
- *Expected*. Though attendance in this class is not mandatory for membership, an ethos exists in the church which makes joining otherwise difficult. New members who do not attend the membership class are the exception rather than the rule.
- *Required*. No one will be granted membership before completing the new member class.

Retention rates increase significantly from level two (encouraged) to level three (expected). Another sizable increase takes place at level four (required). Most church leaders told us that they began a class at level one or two, and slowly transitioned to level three or four over a few or several years. Attendance and participation tended to be spotty at levels one or two.

Lesson # 7: Without a Mission, Churches Wander Aimlessly

We were surprised at the high correlation between mission statements and retention. Churches that effectively close the back door typically have members who can articulate most of the purposes of the church. Pastors and other church leaders understood this phenomenon and, thus, made concerted efforts to educate. This process of education was redundant and perpetual.

Lesson # 8: The Most Potent Mix for Effective Assimilation Was Relationship Evangelism and Sunday School

Sunday School was the most important program for effective assimilation. When Sunday School members, however, began inviting friends, relatives, and coworkers to their classes, the retention rate increased dramatically. When the Sunday School is the front door, the back door closes tightly.

This approach demands accountability, and various churches had different methods of accountability. But the key issue was *expectations*. The more clearly articulated the *expectation* that a Sunday School member invite unchurched persons, the greater the likelihood that such invitations would take place. Many churches had "reward" systems that encouraged church members to invite people to Sunday School.

Lesson # 9: Systematic Visitor Follow-Up Is Critical

Our first study of evangelistic churches found that a regular outreach program is important for evangelistic results. This study somewhat surprisingly informed us that visitor follow-up is also correlated with assimilation.

Several church leaders spoke of abandoning regular outreach ministries because of low participation and the perception that the programs were ineffective. But many of those same leaders told us that the discontinuation of their regular outreach ministry had disastrous effects. Evangelistic effectiveness declined, and assimilation became problematic.

It would seem that a regular outreach program is an "expectation" factor. To dismantle the program lowers expectations and thus lowers the effectiveness in closing the back door.

Lesson # 10: Expository Preaching Enhances Assimilation Effectiveness

Few of the pastors indicated their preaching style was exclusively expository. But the majority responded that expository preaching was their *predominant* preaching style.

The Bible is a "high expectation" book. Any serious student of Scripture cannot escape the demands of discipleship explicit throughout the Bible. Because expository preaching is "text driven," the high expectations of

Scripture are communicated week after week. And the high expectations engender more effective assimilation.

Lesson # 11: New Christians Need Dual Paths

New Christians, like other new members, need to be involved in some type of new member orientation or class. But they also need additional mentoring and discipling. The study earlier showed that only a minority of the churhes had one-to-one mentoring for new members. But we found that this approach resulted in higher assimilation in the churches. One-on-one mentoring can be very effective if the mentor is both willing and capable.

Lesson # 12: The Laity Must Be Unleashed

High-expectation churches are not solo efforts. The churches in our study typically involved a high percentage of the membership in ministry. Such is the nature of a high-expectation church. Membership carries with it the expectation of ministry. And the higher the level of laity involvement, the more likely the members are to remain in the church as productive disciples.

Lesson # 13: The Greeter Ministry Can Be Very Important

We were surprised to discover that a relationship existed between an effective greeter ministry and the closing of the back door. Once again, however, we learned that a ministry that creates an environment of high expectations enhances assimilation. The greeter ministry communicated to everyone, from first-time guests to long-term members, that much is expected of the members.

Lesson # 14: High-Expectation Churches Are Praying Churches

Too little has been said in this book about the importance of prayer and prayer ministries in the churches in this study. A pastor in South Carolina said it best: "We believe in the programs, plans, emphases, and methodologies we attempt in our church. But ultimately we know that our strength is not from ourselves, but from God Himself. That's why our best assimilation ministry is our prayer ministry. Through fervent prayer we show our dependence upon God."

Remember an important statistic cited in chapter 1. We divided the churches in our study into two equal groups. The first group was the least effective in assimilation, and they were thus called "lower-assimilation" churches. The second group represented the 50 percent of the churches that were most effective in assimilation. They were called the "higher assimilation" churches.

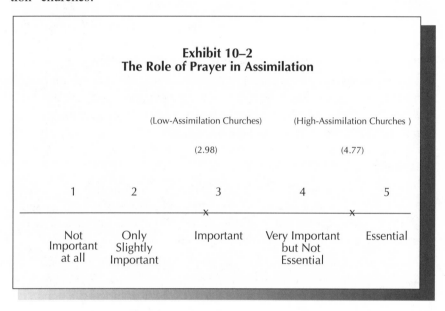

Exhibit 10–2
The Role of Prayer in Assimilation

(Low-Assimilation Churches)   (High-Assimilation Churches)

(2.98)   (4.77)

1	2	3	4	5
Not Important at all	Only Slightly Important	Important	Very Important but Not Essential	Essential

Of the two groups, the higher-assimilation churches regarded prayer as much more critical to the life of the church than the lower-assimilation churches. Those church leaders seeking to close the back door more effectively, take heed—sometimes the beginning of a prayer ministry that involves many people can be the first step toward assimilating new members more effectively.

Conclusion

When you begin a major research project, you start with assumptions and biases. Our research team has asked numerous persons to review our data, with the hopes that our questions and interpretations did not reflect our biases. To the many people who helped in this aspect of the study, thank you for opening our eyes to areas we did not initially see.

Nevertheless, no study is bias free. For any problems with interpretation I, therefore, take full responsibility.

The question is inevitably asked: Were we surprised at any point in the study? The response is always mixed. Some answers we expected. Others were almost totally unexpected. We addressed many of these surprises earlier.

The title of this book reflects the biggest surprise—the correlation between retention and stricter membership requirements seemed to be a theme running through a significant portion of the responses.

Do these responses indicate a trend in the evangelical church in America? Can we expect membership to be more meaningful in the twenty-first century? On the one hand, one could look at our study group and conclude that these churches would not be representative of a trend. After all, only 3–4 percent of the churches in America could have met the evangelistic requirements established by our study.

On the other hand, we have found that these evangelistic churches tend to be trendsetters. We would not be surprised, therefore, to find a significantly developing trend in membership requirements. Could we perhaps become a nation of high-expectation churches?

I conclude this book with two questions and responses. First, are there dangers to becoming a high-expectation church? One clear danger we heard in our postsurvey interviews was the danger of moving a church too fast in this process. "Eating an elephant" is indeed a good strategy. The church leader certainly needs to be in front leading the people of the church. But he does not want to be so far ahead of the people that they mistake him for the enemy and shoot him in the rear!

Another potential danger is moving from high-expectations to legalism. Some church leaders confessed that they led their churches to an extreme position. In their zeal to make church membership meaningful, they developed legalistic attitudes and requirements. Evangelism suffered in this environment.

The second question asks if it is possible for any church to become both evangelistic and high retention. My response is an unequivocal yes.

Please understand that most of the churches in our study were not in rapid-growth demographic locations. Many of the churches had inadequate facilities. And many times the leaders confessed their mistakes and dubious leadership skills.

So what makes these church leaders different from others? How did they lead their churches to growth and effective assimilation? Several words could describe most of the leaders. They were *committed* to their churches. They had a long-term perspective of their ministries where they presently served. Though they were always open to the will of God, they did not try to leave every time a problem developed. They did not suffer from the "greener-grass syndrome."

These leaders were also *persistent*. They did not give up easily. They were willing to take two steps backward to go three steps forward. Because they had a long-term perspective, they were able to see beyond today's setbacks to the victories of tomorrow. The leaders kept focused on major issues and emphasized them when it seemed no one was listening.

Another word that could describe the majority of leaders in the study is *proactive*. They did not seek comfort; rather, they urged people toward commitment. Their proactive leadership sometimes engendered conflict. Although these leaders neither sought nor desired conflict, they did not let the critical voices of a few keep the church from moving forward.

Finally, the leaders of these churches were *prayerful*. They knew that any victory would come from God and Him alone. They depended on Him to meet all their needs. And because they so believed that God would work miracles in their midst, they rarely lost their zeal, vision, or focus.

Please remember, most of the pastors and other leaders of these churches are not common names in the evangelical world. They may never be the pastors of megachurches. Then again, they may very well be. But, above all, they are people who believe that God has called them to their churches and their ministries. And they believe that the best is yet to come.

A pastor from Virginia wrote: "Every time I see what God has done in this church, I stand amazed that He decided to use me. Please tell anyone who will listen that if God can use me, He can use anyone."

Such is my prayer for you, the readers of this book. Whether you are a pastor, staff member, or layperson, I pray that God will use you mightily. I have seen a glimpse of how He is working with some who have sold out to God completely. And I have no doubt that He desires to bless you and your ministry to the fullest.

May God richly bless you. And may you keep pressing on "toward the goal for the prize of the upward call of God in Christ Jesus" (Phil. 3:14).

APPENDIX A

Participating Churches

City	Church	Pastor	Church Setting
Alabama			
Alabaster	Westwood Baptist Church	Jay Gordon	LCS
Anderson	First Baptist Church	Jon Warren	TW
Anniston	Hill Crest Baptist Church	Rick Reaves	MCS
Arley	Arley Baptist Church	Mike Goforth	OC
Athens	Lindsay Lane Baptist Church	Dusty McLemore	MCD
Athens	Round Island Baptist Church	William Bailey	MCS
Auburn	Lakeview Baptist Church	Al Jackson	MCS
Bridgeport	First Baptist Church	Jim Bernard	TW
Excel	Excel Baptist Church	Tom Daniel	TW
Florunia	Johnson Crossroads Baptist Church	Harry W. Underwood	OC
Hueytown	North Highlands Baptist Church	Douglas O'Brien	MCD
Jasper	Blooming Grove Baptist Church	J. Donnell Brown	OC
Locust Fork	Locust Fork Baptist Church	Ronald Foshee	TW
Madison	Wall Highway Baptist Church	Phil Carlisle	OC
Mobile	Cypress Shores Baptist Church	Randy Johnson	LCS
Mobile	First Baptist Church Tillman's Corner	John W. McClendon	MCS

City	Church	Pastor	Church Setting
Newton	Bethel Baptist Church	Allen Norris	OC
Oneonta	Union Hill Baptist Church	Bill Barnett	OC
Pell City	Eden Westside Baptist Church	Jacky Connell	MCS
Prattville	East Memorial Baptist Church	Glenn Graham Jr.	MCS
Samson	Piney Grove Baptist Church	Randall H. Taylor	TW
Wetumpka	Santuck Baptist Church	Morgan Bailey	OC
Arkansas			
Chandler	Corona Baptist Church	Byron Banta	LCS
Des Arc	First Baptist Church	Melvin York	TW
El Dorado	Second Baptist Church	Dwain Miller	MCS
Hensley	Forest Tower Baptist Church	J. W. Kocourek	OC
Lake City	First Baptist Church	Mike McDaniel	TW
Lavaca	First Baptist Church	Grant C. Ethridge	TW
Paragould	Southside Baptist Church	Troy Gramling	MCS
Pearcy	Pearcy Baptist Church	Leroy Wagner	OC
Searcy	Trinity Baptist Church	Michael Hulsey	MCS
Thatcher	First Southern Baptist Church	Gene Barnett	SM
West Helena	Second Baptist Church	Rudy Davis	MCD
Yuma	Morningside Baptist Church	Gilbert K. Taeger	LCS
California			
Bakersfield	Panama Baptist Church	Larry Dotson	OC
Carlsbad	First Baptist Church	Gary Harr	MCD
Ceres	Emmanuel Baptist Church	Rudy Schreiber	LCD
Corona	Olive Branch Community Church	Dwight Riddle	LCS
Fremont	Alder Avenue Baptist Church	Mark Milwee	LCS

City	Church	Pastor	Church Setting
Hespenia	First Baptist Church	Wayne Stockstill	LCS
Livermore	Trinity Baptist Church	Jim Meek	LCS
Sacramento	Hillsdale Blvd. Baptist Church	Clifford A. Sims	MCS
San Diego	First Baptist Church of Mira Mesa	Dwight Simpson	LCS
Vallejo	North Hills Baptist Church	William E. Dodson	LCS
Colorado			
Colorado Springs	Pleasant Valley Baptist Church	Tim Gotchey	LCS
Denver	Riverside Baptist Church	Tom Armstrong	LCD
Monte Vista	Calvary Baptist Church	Richard Nettles	SM
Sterling	Emmanuel Baptist Church	Rick Lewis	MCD
Westminster	First Southern Baptist Church	Ed Gatlin	LCS
Connecticut			
Litchfield	Friendship Baptist Church	Darril Deaton	SM
Florida			
Arcadia	Calvary Baptist Church	Lance C. Beckham	SM
Brandon	Bell Shoals Baptist Church	John Russell	LCS
Callahan	First Baptist Church of Gray Gables	Chris Drum	OC
Ft. Lauderdale	Riverland Baptist Church	Ron Mensinger	LCS
Gainesville	Southwest Baptist Mission Church	Chuck Gass	LCD
Gulf Breeze	Midway Baptist Church	Dennis J. Brunet	SM
Interlachen	First Baptist Church	James Roberson	TW
Jacksonville	Fruit Cove Baptist Church	Tim Maynard	OC
Jacksonville	New Life Baptist Church	Alan McCurdy	LCS
Jacksonville	San Jose Baptist Church	Matthew Meadows	LCS

City	Church	Pastor	Church Setting
Lake City	Huntsville Baptist Church	Tom Watson	OC
Largo	First Baptist Church of Indian Rocks	Ken Moody	LCS
Madison	Fellowship Baptist Church	Steve McHorgue	SM
Mary Esther	First Baptist Church	Joe Plott	MCD
Mayo	Pleasant Grove Baptist Church	Randy Waters	SM
Miami	First Baptist Church of Perrina	Jay Hancock	LCS
Miami	Iglesia Bautista Resurreccion	Emanuel Roque	LCS
Middleburg	First Baptist Church	Danny Bennett	OC
Mims	Mission Baptist Church	S. Dennis Wilbanks	MCS
Naples	First Baptist Church of Naples	Todd McMichen	LCS
Niceville	Rocky Bayou Baptist Church	Larry W. Corder	MCS
Okeechobee	Oakview Baptist Church	John W. Keith	SM
Okeechobee	Treasure Island Baptist Church	John A. Giddens III	MCS
Oviedo	First Baptist Church	Dwayne E. Mercer and Louise Howard	LCS
Palmetto	Tenth Street Baptist Church	Anne Tabor	SM
Perry	New Home Baptist Church	Bill Jenkins	MCS
Port St. Joe	First Baptist Church	Gary Smith	SM
Sarasota	Southside Baptist Church	R. Wayne Bright	LCD
Spring Hill	Northcliffe Baptist Church	Jerry Waugh	MCS
Starke	Hope Baptist Church	Eugene V. Coons	OC
Tampa	Belmont Baptist Church	David P. Rice	LCS
Titusville	Westside Baptist Church	Rocky Purvis	MCS
Georgia			
Adel	New Life Baptist Church	Harris Whitman	OC

City	Church	Pastor	Church Setting
Baxley	Ten Mile Creek Baptist Church	Mark Bordeaux	OC
Blackshear	Emmanuel Baptist Church	E. Donald Hattaway	SM
Canton	Hopewell Baptist Church	Norman R. Hunt	OC
Dacula	Hebron Baptist Church	Larry Wynn	TW
Dalton	Liberty Baptist Church	Scott Crow	MCS
Dalton	Macedonia Baptist Church	Steve Fluckhart	OC
Douglasville	Chapel Hill Road Baptist Church	T. Mark Lively	LCS
Douglasville	Sunset Hills Baptist Church	R. C. Watson	LCS
Ellerslie	Ellerslie Baptist Church	David Long	TW
Fleming	Fleming Baptist Church	Jim G. Wilson	OC
Gainesville	Grace Baptist Church	Chuck Nation	MCS
Hazlehurst	Southside Baptist Church	Ben Glosson	SM
Hinesville	Faith Baptist Church	Richard Fox	MCS
Marietta	Shady Grove Baptist Church	Charles S. Callahan	MCD
Martinez	Baker Woods Baptist Church	Ellis Moore	LCS
Midway	Midway First Baptist Church	William T. Horstmeyer	TW
Rome	Calvary Baptist Church	Frank G. Wood	MCS
Rossville	South Rossville Baptist Church	Eddy G. Rushing	LCS
St. Marys	First Baptist Church	Bob Halstead Jr.	MCS
Stockbridge	Metro Heights Baptist Church	Arthur Nelson	N/A
Villa Rica	New Georgia Baptist Church	Roy Crowe	OC
Illinois			
Centralia	Eternity Baptist Church	Karl Barnfield	MCD
Chicago	Bread of Life Missionary Baptist Church	Leon Johnson	LCD
Chicago	Faith Tabernacle Baptist Church	Donald L. Sharp	LCS

City	Church	Pastor	Church Setting
Chicago	Mission of Faith Baptist Church	Eugene L. Gibson Sr.	LCD
Matteson	New Faith Baptist Church	Frank Thomas	MCS
Olney	Olney Southern Baptist Church	Les Mason	SM
Sullivan	Bible Baptist Church	Matt Underwood	OC

Indiana

City	Church	Pastor	Church Setting
Fort Wayne	Greater Come As You Are Baptist Church	Anthony Payton	LCD

Kansas

City	Church	Pastor	Church Setting
Salina	First Southern Baptist Church	R. Glenn Davis	MCD

Kentucky

City	Church	Pastor	Church Setting
Campbellsville	Elk Horn Baptist Church	Daniel S. Hunt Sr.	OC
Covington	South Side Baptist Church	A. Harold Pike	LCD
Frankfort	Buck Run Baptist Church	Robert H. Jackson	OC
Lexington	Gardenside Baptist Church	Ron Fellemende	LCS
Louisville	Springdale Church	David Butler	LCS
Owensboro	Walnut Memorial Baptist Church	Odell Beauchamp	MCS
Shepherdsville	Mount Elmira Baptist Church	Curtis Tucker	OC
Williamsburg	Mountain Ash Baptist Church	Billy Carpenter	OC

Louisiana

City	Church	Pastor	Church Setting
Franklinton	Hillcrest Baptist Church	H. Gene Richards	SM
Haughton	Koran Baptist Church	George Rogers	OC
Kentwood	Spring Creek Baptist Church	Danny R. Smith	OC
Mandeville	First Baptist Church	Ken Schroeder	MCS
Monroe	Loch Arbor Baptist Church	James A. Myrick	OC
Pineville	Trinity Baptist Church	Wayne Kite	MCD

184

City	Church	Pastor	Church Setting
Massachusetts			
Cambridge	Berkland Baptist Church	Paul Kim	LCD
Maryland			
Baltimore	Catonsville Baptist Church	Bob Lilly	LCS
Bowie	Cresthill Baptist Church	James E. Painter	MCS
Fort Washington	Fort Foote Baptist Church	Joseph W. Lyles	LCS
Frederick	South End Baptist Church	Ken Stalls	LCD
Port Deposit	Pleasant View Baptist Church	Harold M. Phillips	OC
Silver Springs	Global Mission Church of Greater Washington	Jei W. Kim	LCS
Sykesville	Elders Baptist Church	Kenny Heath	MCS
Michigan			
Flushing	Westside Baptist Church	Randy Wheeler	LCS
Jackson	Gorham Baptist Church	Jerry Bailey	MCS
Missouri			
Anderson	Patterson Heights Baptist Church	A. C. Sam Mitchell	OC
Branson	Victor Baptist Church	Kenny Robinette	OC
Desloge	Cantwell Baptist Church	Gregory L. McCord	SM
Excelsior Springs	Pisgah Baptist Church	R. J. Adrain	MCS
Greenwood	First Baptist Church	Steve Hartwich	MCS
Holt	Northern Hills Baptist Church	Richard Hubbard	SM
Mt. Vernon	Covenant Baptist Church	Kathryn Maberry and Mark Killingsworth	SM
Salem	Oak Grove Baptist Church	John A. Smith	SM
Springfield	Springhill Baptist Church	Kenny Qualls	OC

City	Church	Pastor	Church Setting
Washington	First Baptist Church	Chuck Williams	MCD
Waynesville	Westside Baptist Church	Lee Schaffer	MCS

Mississippi

City	Church	Pastor	Church Setting
Louisville	Good Hope Baptist Church	Noel Dear	OC
Petal	Greens Creek Baptist Church	Mike Routon	SM
Southaven	Carriage Hills Baptist Church	Bradley D. Spellman	MCS
Southaven	Trinity Baptist Church	Jim Butler	LCS
Tishomingo	Tishomingo Baptist Church	William Burge	OC
Tupelo	East Heights Baptist Church	Mike Hatfield	MCS
Tupelo	Harrisburg Baptist Church	Bo Grace	MCS
Union	Antioch Baptist Church	James Young	OC
Vicksburg	Goodrum Memorial Baptist Church	Thomas G. Simmons	MCS

Montana

City	Church	Pastor	Church Setting
Billings	Rimrock Baptist Church	John F. Hunn	LCS

North Carolina

City	Church	Pastor	Church Setting
Charlotte	Mecklenburg Community Church	James E. White	LCS
Claremont	First Baptist Church	Dennis J. Richards Sr.	SM
Concord	Young Memorial Baptist Church	Jeff Smith	MCS
Creedmoor	First Baptist Church	Don Brown	TW
Fayetteville	LaGrange Park Baptist Church	David S. George	MCS
Grover	Patterson Springs Baptist Church	Steve Waters	TW
Icard	First Baptist Church	Bobby Earls	TW
Kings Mountain	Macedonia Baptist Church	David A. Phillbeck	OC
Lumberton	Smyrna Baptist Church	Charles P. Locklear	OC

City	Church	Pastor	Church Setting
Midway Park	Enon Chapel Baptist Church	James Kelley	LCS
Morganton	Burkemont Baptist Church	Marshall Pridgen Jr.	OC
Sanford	East Sanford Baptist Church	William M. Runion	MCD
Stanley	Lucia Baptist Church	Michael Davis	TW
Wilmington	Lake Forest Baptist Church	Ralph Holt	MCS

North Dakota

Bismarck	Riverwood Baptist Church	Ronald K. Rich	LCS

Nebraska

Bellevue	First Baptist Church	Ron Elliot	MCD
Lincoln	New Covenant Community Church	Boyd Pelley	LCS

New Mexico

Deming	Bethel Baptist Church	A. Kerry Chadwick	MCD

Nevada

Henderson	First Southern Baptist Church	Rene Joseph Houle	LCD
Henderson	Highland Hills Baptist Church	John Mark Simmons	LCS
Las Vegas	First Baptist Church	Richard B. Johnson	LCD
Sun Valley	First Baptist Church	Roland Lackey	MCS

New York

Rome	One Heart Church	David Pope	OC

Ohio

Camden	First Southern Baptist Church	Greg Jackson	TW
Cincinnati	Clough Pike Baptist Church	Stephen Anthony	MCS
Dayton	Grace Baptist Church	Douglas G. Criswell	LCS

City	Church	Pastor	Church Setting
Grove City	First Baptist Church	Jerry L. Neal	MCS
Lebanon	Urbancrest Baptist Church	Tom Pendergrass	MCS
Maineville	Fellowship Baptist Church	Gary W. Stringer	OC
Mentor	Trinity Baptist Church	Gerald Bontrager	LCS
Mt. Orab	First Baptist Church	Bob D. Hatcher	TW
New Carlisle	First Baptist Church	Rick Shoemaker	SM
Norwood	New Bethel Baptist Church	Kirk Pike	LCD
Pataskala	Jersey Baptist Church	Phil Duncan	OC
Oklahoma			
Altus	Emmanuel Baptist Church	Boyd Whitehead	MCS
Blanchard	Midway Southern Baptist Church	Charlene Allison	OC
Cushing	Oak Grove Baptist Church	Jackie Allen	OC
Estacada	Clackanas Valley Baptist Church	Bill Griggs	OC
Hugo	Oak Grove Baptist Church	Hershel Reed	OC
Jenks	Beaver Street Baptist Church	Vernon D. Liles	SM
Kellyville	First Baptist Church	Doug Miller	TW
Lawton	Cameron Baptist Church	Mike Teel	LCS
Noble	Twelve Corners Baptist Church	David Henson	OC
Oklahoma City	Agnew Avenue Baptist Church	Larry Chapmon	LCS
Okmulgee	Second Baptist Church	Bob Burch	MCS
Panola	Panola Baptist Church	Douglas R. Wilkins	OC
Park Hill	First Baptist Church	Andy Bowman	OC
Picher	First Baptist Church	Wayne L. Wall	TW
Sallisaw	Immanuel Baptist Church	John H. Ewart	SM
Terlton	First Baptist Church	Louis R. Speck	OC

City	Church	Pastor	Church Setting
Yukon	Trinity Baptist Church	Scott Kinney	MCS
Pennsylvania			
W. Reading	Northside Baptist Church	Edward B. H. Johnson	MCD
South Carolina			
Aiken	Lighthouse Baptist Church	Marion Britton	OC
Bamberg	First Baptist Church	Charlie Barnard	TW
Belton	Cedar Shoals Baptist Church	Randy Harling	OC
Lugoff	Lugoff Fellowship Baptist Church	C. Bruce Watford	MCD
Monks Corner	Cordesville Baptist Church	Randy A. Woods Sr.	SM
Mt. Pleasant	East Cooper Baptist Church	Craig Harris	MCS
Ridgeland	Great Swamp Baptist Church	Kenneth D. Busbee	OC
Summerville	Oakbrook Baptist Church	George M. Rossi	MCS
Sumter	Shaw Heights Baptist Church	Victor L. Cheek	LCS
W. Columbia	Agape Baptist Church	Bill Howard	MCS
Walhudla	Open Door Baptist Church	Jimmy Boggs	SM
South Dakota			
Rapid City	Rapid Valley Baptist Church	A. L. Davis	MCS
Tennessee			
Bartlett	Faith Baptist Church	Danny Sinquefield	LCS
Celina	First Baptist Church	Doug Plumlee	TW
Clarksville	Greater Missionary Baptist Church	Willie J. Freeman	LCS
Clarksville	Hillcrest Baptist Church	Larry G. Mulberry	LCS
Finley	Finley Baptist Church	Charles Halliburton	OC
Lebanon	Hillcrest Baptist Church	Glenn Denton	MCS

City	Church	Pastor	Church Setting
Manchester	Trinity Baptist Church	Kerry Walker	SM
Morristown	Alpha Baptist Church	Thomas R. James	MCS
Munford	Munford Baptist Church	M. Todd Wilson	TW
Murfreesboro	Mt. Hermon Baptist Church	Richard Graham	OC
Palmyra	Bethel Baptist Church	Ted Denny	OC
Rutledge	Blue Springs Baptist Church	Don Edwards	OC
Smyrna	First Baptist Church	Eddie Mosley	MCS
Spring City	First Baptist Church	Steve Pearson	SM
Thompson Station	Thompson Station Baptist Church	Tom McCoy	TW
Union City	Pleasant Hill Baptist Church	Jimmy Brown	OC
Union City	Sunswept Baptist Church	James A. Kinsey	MCD
White House	First Baptist Church	Leslie L. Bruce	SM
Whitesburg	Highland Baptist Church	Terry Bunch	OC

Texas

City	Church	Pastor	Church Setting
Adkins	Salem Sayers Baptist Church	Tony Romans	LCS
Amarillo	Mescalero Baptist Church	Roy Almaroad	OC
Azle	First Baptist Church	Paul K. Wilson	MCS
Brenham	First Baptist Church	Steve Ponder	MCD
Burkburnett	Central Baptist Church	Alec Haigood	MCD
Celeste	First Baptist Church	James Ralson	TW
Comanchee	Eastside Baptist Church	Don Longoria	SM
Corpus Christi	Calallen Baptist Church	Ted Eaton	LCS
Del Rio	Northside Baptist Church	Bob Lockhart	MCS
Denison	Hyde Park Baptist Church	Mark Mitchell	MCD

City	Church	Pastor	Church Setting
Dripping Springs	First Baptist Church	David W. Smith	TW
Electra	Hillside Baptist Church	Bob Webb	SM
Flower Mound	First Baptist Church	David Williams	MCS
Grand Prairie	Inglewood Baptist Church	J. R. Chaney	LCS
Greenville	Dixon Baptist Church	Jimmy Vaughn	OC
Houston	Anchor Baptist Church	Lee McDowell	LCS
Houston	First Baptist Church	Don Kidd	MCS
Huntsville	Northside Baptist Church	Reagan M. Cooksey	OC
Katy	The Fellowship at Cinco Ranch	Jerry Edmonson	LCS
Killeen	Memorial Baptist Church	Joe Rich	LCS
Lake Dallas	First Baptist Church	Andy Kennedy	SM
LaPorte	Bayshore Baptist Church	Stan Jordan	LCS
Lufkin	Faith Baptist Church	Elton Musick	SM
Madisonville	First Baptist Church	Charles Higgs	SM
Nederland	Hillcrest Baptist Church	Elvin Gibson	MCS
New Braunfels	Oakwood Baptist Church	Roxi Vanstory	MCS
New Caney	Forestwood Baptist Church	Eric Scott	TW
Palacios	First Baptist Church	Hollas Hoffman	SM
Palestine	Westwood Baptist Church	Robert O. Rachuig	MCD
Pleasanton	First Baptist Church	Jeff Williams	SM
San Antonio	Alamo City Christian Fellowship	Dick Dickson	LCD
San Antonio	Castle Hills First Baptist Church	Malcolm Grainger	LCS
Tyler	Hopewell Baptist Church	Dennis E. Terry Sr.	OC
Victoria	Parkway Baptist Church	Scott Weatherford	LCS

City	Church	Pastor	Church Setting
Virginia			
Bassett	Orchard Drive Baptist Church	Richard C. Clark	TW
Colonial Heights	Colonial Heights Baptist Church	Ronald A. West	MCD
Hampton	Newmarket Baptist Church	S. E. Hathaway	LCS
Hopewell	Woodlawn Baptist Church	Kenneth Hendricks	MCS
Ladysmith	Ladysmith Baptist Church	Roger Gorby	OC
Midlothian	Swift Creek Baptist Church	Phillip Hunt	MCS
Spotsylvania	Travelers Rest Baptist Church	Clyde H. Coleman	OC
Wirtz	Halesford Baptist Church	Melvin J. Harris	OC
West Virginia			
Airway Heights	First Baptist Church	E. Robert Cassels	TW
Berkeley Springs	Berkeley Baptist Church	John Gilbert	TW
Lakewood	First Baptist Church	Walt Kelley Jr.	LCD
Shepherdstown	Covenant Baptist Church	Ron Larson	OC

*Church Setting Codes

OC - Open country / rural area
TW - Town (500 to 2,499 people)
SM - Small city (2,500 to 9,999 people)
MCS - Medium city / downtown (10,000 to 49,999 people)
MCS - Medium city / suburbs (10,000 to 49,999 people)
LCD - Large city / downtown or inner city (50,000 + people)
LCS - Large city / suburbs (50,000 + people)

Survey Instrument

I. BASIC CHURCH INFORMATION

Church name _____

Street address _____

City_____ State _____Zip_____

Phone: **Day** (__) _____ **Evening** (__)_____

Fax (if applicable)

Age of the church (the number of years the church has been in existence as a constituted body): _____

Name of person completing this survey:

Position held in the church:

Phone # (if needed to clarify responses):

A. Please use the information from your *1993–94* and *1994–95* Annual Church Profiles or your church minutes to complete the following information. If your church does not keep records for the following categories, please mark N/A.

	1993–94	1994–95	N/A
1. Resident membership	_____	_____	_____
2. Nonresident membership	_____	_____	_____
3. Average A.M. worship attendance	_____	_____	_____
4. Average P.M. worship attendance	_____	_____	_____
5. Average Sunday School attendance	_____	_____	_____
6. Total additions by baptism	_____	_____	_____
7. Total additions by letter	_____	_____	_____
8. Total of *ALL* additions	_____	_____	_____
9. Total losses by transfer to another church in the same area	_____	_____	_____
10. Total losses by "reversion" (members who just "drop out" and are not attending church anywhere)	_____	_____	_____

11. What percentage of the church's baptisms in 1994–95 were persons who were not previously affiliated with *any* church?   _____%

12. What percentage of the church's baptisms in 1994–95 were persons who were not previously affiliated with *your* church? _____%

B. We recognize the difficulty of estimating the level of church participation of each church member. However, please estimate the following percentages

13. Average percentage of Sunday A.M. worship attenders who are:
    13a. First-time guests. . . . . _____%
    13b. Regular attenders (at least 50% of the A.M. services
    a month), but who are *not* church members . . . . _____%
    13c. Church members who attend fewer than 50% of A.M.
    services each month . . . . _____%
    13d. Church members who attend more than 50% of A.M.
    services each month . . . . _____%
    13e. Church members who attend Sunday School and a
    minimum of one service per week at least 50% of the time. . . . . _____%
    13f. Church members who hold a position/task in the
    church (including any elected position in the church) . . . . _____%
    13g. Church members who regularly attend Sunday School
    and at least one service per week, who hold a position in the church,
    and who financially support the church on a regular basis . . . . _____%
14. What percentage of members *who have joined within the last year*
    now attend Sunday School and one service per week at least
    50% of the time? _____%
15. What percentage of first-time guests return for a second visit? _____%
16. Does your church have an organized system for keeping record of the above statistics?
    Yes _____   No _____

C. Please provide the following geographic and demographic information about the church.

17. Church setting:
    _____a. Open country/rural area
    _____b. Town (500–2,499 people)
    _____c. Small city (2,500–9,999 people)
    _____d. Medium city/downtown (10,000–49,999 people)
    _____e. Medium city/suburbs (10,000–49,999 people)
    _____f. Large city/downtown or inner city (50,000+ people)
    _____g. Large city/suburbs (50,000+ people)
18. Congregational demographics of *resident* membership

Race		Age		Economic Levels	
Caucasian	_____%	Under 18	_____%	Upper class	_____%
African-American	_____%	19–35	_____%	Middle class	_____%
Hispanic	_____%	36–50	_____%	Lower class	_____%
Asian	_____%	51–65	_____%		100%
Other	_____%	66+	_____%		
	100%		100%		

II. CHURCH STAFF INFORMATION

19. Senior pastor's name: _____

20. Senior pastor's highest education level:

_____a. High school   _____c. Seminary (Master's)

_____b. College   _____d. Seminary (Doctoral)

                                      _____e. Seminary studies (no degree)

21. Is the senior pastor full-time?   Yes _____   No _____

22. How long has the senior pastor served at the church?   Years _____   Months _____

23. For each of the following preaching styles, estimate the percentage of the senior pastor's sermons that reflect that style:

    a. *Expository.* Primarily explanation or commentary on the biblical text; expounds the central idea of the text; often includes preaching through a book of the Bible.

    b. *Topical.* Difficult to define; typically, a sermon built around a topic, with biblical application to that topic.

    c. *Thematic.* Usually a series of sermons developed around a central theme or idea; does not typically involve preaching through a book of the Bible.

    d. *Narrative.* Story form that, from the beginning to end, develops the plot of the story as a theme; a biblical truth presented in parable form.

24. Which of the following ministry/pastoral/administrative tasks does the senior pastor find most exciting and challenging? Least exciting and challenging? Please mark two tasks in each column.

Most Exciting	**Least Exciting**
_____a. Pastoral care	_____a. Pastoral care
_____b. Preaching	_____b. Preaching
_____c. Administration	_____c. Administration
_____d. Discipleship/training members	_____d. Discipleship/ training members
_____e. Evangelism	_____e. Evangelism
_____f. Building campaigns	_____f. Building campaigns
_____g. Visitation	_____g. Visitation
_____h. Goal setting	_____h. Goal setting
_____i. Committee meetings	_____i. Committee meetings
_____j. Budgeting	_____j. Budgeting
_____k. Future planning	_____k. Future planning
_____l. Staff leadership	_____l. Staff leadership
_____m. Other: _____	_____m. Other: _____

25. Which of the following descriptions best illustrates the senior pastor's leadership style? Please mark only *one* of the responses.

_____a.	*High task/high relationship*	Emphasizes both relationships with people and "getting things done"; a *team captain* who participates in the game.
_____b.	*High task/low relationship*	Higher interest in production and "getting things done" than in relationships with people; a *commander* who pushes others to reach goals.
_____c.	*Low task/high relationship*	Emphasizes people, feelings, and fellowship more than "getting things done"; a *caregiver* who primarily ministers to his congregation.
_____d.	*Low task/low relationship*	Focuses little on developing relationships or on "getting things done"; a *recluse* who often retreats from the leadership role.

26. Using the following scale, circle the *number* that best signifies the senior pastor's leadership style related to change:

1	2	3	4	5	6	7	8
Sustaining: Tends to work to preserve the status quo; little willingless to change			*Reactionary:* Responds to needs, willing to change, but typically addresses needs only when they become apparent			*Visionary:* Often recognizes needs before they are apparent to others; leads in planning to meet the needs; encourages change when needed	

27. Briefly describe the senior pastor's steps/principles/policies for leading the church through change.

28. How does your church typically respond to a challenge to change?
____a. Usually unwilling to change, regardless of the issue.
____b. Reluctant to change; changes grudgingly only when forced by circumstances.
____c. Reluctant to change, but will do so when adequate study, prayer, and leadership support the need to change; change typically occurs slowly.
____d. Open to change as long as adequate study, prayer, and leadership support the need to change.
____e. Willing to change simply because leadership suggests the change is necessary.
____f. Other: _____

29. Using the following scale, please rate the level of influence of each of these factors on the senior pastor's development as a leader.

1	2	3	4	5
Not an Influence	A Slight Influence	An Important Influence	A Very Important Influence, but Not a Most Significant Influence	A Most Significant Influence

    ____a. Leadership training in college or seminary

    ____b. Example of a mentor

    ____c. Participation in leadership conferences

    ____d. Experiences of failure in church work

    ____e. Bible studies about leaders

    ____f. Experiences of success in church work

    ____g. Books on leadership

    ____h. A leadership expert, such as John Maxwell

    ____i. Other: _____

III. THE CHURCH'S UNDERSTANDING OF ASSIMILATION

Assimilation—the incorporation of individuals into a local church so that they have a sense of belonging and are involved in the ministry of that local church.

30. Is a staff member (other than the pastor) or a layperson primarily responsible for directing the church's assimilation efforts?　　　　　　　Yes _____　　No _____

Other staff member:　　　or　　　　　　Layperson:

a. Title: _____

b. Full-time?　　　　　_____Yes
　　　　　　　　　　　_____No

c. Approximate number of hours per week devoted to assimilation:　　_____

d. Position: _____

e. Approximate number of hours per week devoted to assimilation:　　_____

31. Define *evangelism* as your church understands the term:

32. Please describe in some detail what your church believes must take place for a person to be "saved."

33. Briefly describe the senior pastor's understanding of his role and responsibility in the church's assimilation program.

34. Please list the guidelines you use to determine if a church member has been successfully assimilated into your church, i.e., how do you know when a member has "a sense of belonging and is thus involved in the ministry of the church"?

35. Is your church a "cell group" church, defined as a church whose primary small groups are typically nontraditional, off-campus groups with primary responsibilities of accountability, fellowship, and study? Typically, worship in this church is a "celebration" of the combined cell groups.

_____Yes _____No

36. Using the scale below, please rank the importance of each of the following programs/ministries to the church's overall **assimilation** process. If your church does not offer this type of ministry/program, please mark N/A. Please remember that you are rating these programs on their importance to your *assimilation* program.

1	2	3	4	5
Not Important at All	Only Slightly Important	Important	Very Important but Not Essential	Essential

36a.	_____A.M. worship	36v.	_____Wednesday night service
36b.	_____P.M. worship	36w.	_____Visitation program
36c.	_____Music program	36x.	_____Preschool programs
36d.	_____Children's programs	36y.	_____Youth programs
36e.	_____Family ministries	36z.	_____Senior adult ministries
36f.	_____Sunday School	36aa.	_____Woman's Missionary Union
36g.	_____Brotherhood group	36bb.	_____Promise Keepers
36h.	_____Support groups	36cc.	_____Recreational activities
36i.	_____Preaching	36dd.	_____Discipleship Training
36j.	_____Doctrinal studies	36ee.	_____Outreach Bible studies
36k.	_____Prayer groups	36ff.	_____Ethnic ministries
36l.	_____Social ministries	36gg.	_____Cell groups
36m.	_____Bus ministry	36hh.	_____Special events
36n.	_____Saturday worship	36ii.	_____Mission studies/trips
36o.	_____Day-care program	36jj.	_____Weekday programs
36p.	_____New member's class	36kk.	_____Church-affiliated school
36q.	_____Women's ministries school	36ll.	_____Target evangelism
36r.	_____Contemporary worship	36mm.	_____One-to-one discipling
36s.	_____Seeker services	36nn.	_____Children's worship
36t.	_____Single adult ministry	36oo.	_____Other:
36u.	_____Bible study groups		

37. At this point in your church's life, what is your evaluation of the church's overall effectiveness in assimilation?
    _____a. Very poor/not effective at all
    _____b. Poor/only slightly effective
    _____c. Fair/somewhat effective
    _____d. Good/effective
    _____e. Excellent/very effective

IV. THE CHURCH'S MISSION/VISION/DIRECTION

Mission—the primary purposes in which all Christian churches should be involved; these purposes typically include worship, evangelism, discipleship, ministry, and fellowship.

Vision—God's *specific* plan for a *specific* church at a *specific* time.

38. If the church has a *mission* statement, what is that statement?

_____a. The church does not have a mission statement.

_____b. The church has a mission statement that reads as follows:

39. If the church has a mission statement, how important is the statement in the life of the congregation?

    _____a. Very important

    _____b. Important

    _____c. Slightly important

    _____d. Not important

    _____e. The church does not have a mission/purpose statement.

40. Does the church have a clearly articulated *vision* statement? _____Yes _____No

41. If your church has a *vision* statement, what is that statement? _____N/A

42. How was the church's vision "discovered," i.e., what steps did the church take to determine God's direction for your congregation?   _____N/A

43. Which of the following obstacles did you face in developing a vision statement? Please mark all that apply.

    _____a. *Tradition*: "We've never needed a vision statement before."

    _____b. *Fear of change*: "Will our church or its programs change if we adopt a vision?"

    _____c. *Complacency*: "We're happy the way we are."

    _____d. *Present focus*: "We've got too many needs right now to begin thinking about what God wants us to do beyond today."

    _____e. *Perceived lack of laborers*: "Where will we get the workers to accomplish these tasks?"

    _____f. *Power struggles*: "Will I begin to lose my position/authority in the church if we adopt a new vision?"

    _____g. *Cost*: "How will we pay for everything our new vision demands?"

    _____h. None of the above

    _____i. Other: _____

44. What changes occurred in the church after the church discovered its "vision"?

_____N/A

45. How is the church's vision and/or mission statement communicated to the congregation and guests? Please mark all that apply.

_____ a.	Sermons	_____ f.	Media advertisement
_____ b.	Church brochure	_____ g.	Bible study classes
_____ c.	Letters from staff	_____ h.	Church bulletin
_____ d.	Newsletter	_____ i.	Church letterhead
_____ e.	Church sign	_____ j.	Worship announcements
		_____ k.	Other: _____

V. VISITORS AND VISITATION

46. Why do first-time guests visit your church? Please rank the three most common motivations given, with one (1) being the highest:
   ____a. The guest heard about the church's good reputation in the community.
   ____b. A friend/family member/coworker invited the guest.
   ____c. The church's location was convenient.
   ____d. The guest heard about the church's programs/ministries.
   ____e. The guest attended a special event at the church.
   ____f. A church advertisement caught the guest's attention.
   ____g. The pastor's preaching ministry attracted the guest.
   ____h. Other: _____

47. If your church has a systematic plan for greeting visitors, please describe that plan.
   ____a. Our church does not have an established plan for greeting guests.
   ____b. Our church does have a plan that includes assigned greeters in the following locations:

_____Parking lot	_____Welcome center
_____Front door only	_____Sunday School classes
_____All entrance doors	_____Worship service
	_____ Other: _____

48. What plan does your church use to recognize guests in a worship service?

49. Does your church have a systematic program for visitor follow-up?
   ____a. Our church does not have a systematic program for visitor follow-up.
   ____b. Our church does have a systematic plan that includes the following:
   _____ (1) Personal letter from the pastor
   _____ (2) Personal letter from other staff

_____ (3) Personal letter from a layperson
_____ (4) Telephone call from the pastor
_____ (5) Telephone call from other staff
_____ (6) Telephone call from a layperson
_____ (7) Personal visit from the pastor
_____ (8) Personal visit from other staff
_____ (9) Personal visit from a layperson
_____ (10) A visitor's packet that includes the following items:

_____ (11) Other: _____

50. If your church has an established time for churchwide visitation, when does it occur?

Sunday	_____	Daytime	_____	Weekly	_____
Monday	_____	Evening	_____	Monthly	_____
Tuesday	_____		_____	Other:	_____
Wednesday	_____				
Thursday	_____				
Friday	_____				
Saturday	_____				

The church does not have an established time for visitation. Instead, we use the following plan:

51. What *specific* opportunities does your church provide for visitors to meet and interact with church staff and church members (for example, a reception for guests after a worship service)?

52. Does your church provide specific parking spaces for guests?   _____ Yes   _____ No

53. Does your church reserve specific seating for guests?   _____ Yes   _____ No

VI. CHURCH MEMBERSHIP REQUIREMENTS/EXPECTATIONS

54. Which of the following are requirements for membership in your church, and which are more expectations than requirements?

		Required	Expected, but Not Required or Expected	Not Required or Expected
54a.	Personal relationship with Christ/salvation experience	_____	_____	_____
54b.	Postconversion counseling with a trained follow-up counselor	_____	_____	_____
54c.	Public testimony of conversion before a committee or the church body	_____	_____	_____
54d.	Baptism by immersion in a Baptist church	_____	_____	_____
54e.	Baptism by immersion in a Southern Baptist church	_____	_____	_____
54f.	Baptism by immersion following a salvation experience, but not necessarily in a Baptist church	_____	_____	_____
54g.	Attendance in a new member/orientation class	_____	_____	_____
54h.	Signed membership covenant that is renewed annually	_____	_____	_____
54i.	Signed membership covenant that is *not* renewed annually	_____	_____	_____
54j.	Commitment to attend a discipling program	_____	_____	_____
54k.	Commitment to spiritual gifts development and eventual service in a ministry of the church	_____	_____	_____
54l.	Commitment to tithe to the church	_____	_____	_____
54m.	Commitment to give financially to the church, but not necessarily to give a tithe	_____	_____	_____
54n.	Regular attendance in worship services	_____	_____	_____
54o.	Regular attendance in a Sunday School class	_____	_____	_____
54p.	Participation in a small-group ministry	_____	_____	_____
54q.	Commitment to follow a specific theological guideline (e.g. *The Baptist Faith and Message* or a local church standard)	_____	_____	_____
54r.	Other: _____	_____	_____	_____

55. Do you require any training for new converts prior to their baptism into the church?

Yes ____ No ____

56. If training is required prior to baptism, what type of training is offered?
57. What requirements or age limitations, if any, does your church place on the baptism of children?
58. Does your church require new members to attend a new member/orientation course?

Yes _____ No _____

59. If the church requires this course, what is the title employed for the class? N/A ___
60. If you require a new member/orientation class, must the course be completed *before* new members are accepted by vote into the church? Yes ___ No ___

N/A _____

61. If your church requires attendance at a new member/orientation class, who teaches the course?

_____a. Senior pastor _____c. Layperson

_____b. Staff member _____d. Other_____

_____e. N/A

62. Are prospects and visitors permitted and/or encouraged to attend the new member/orientation course?

_____Permitted _____Encouraged _____Neither _____N/A

63. When does the new member/orientation course meet?

Day_____ Time_____:_____ No. of weeks_____

64. Which of the following topics are addressed in the new member/orientation class? Please mark all that apply.
_____a. Doctrine of the church
_____b. Polity and government of your church
_____c. History of your church
_____d. Requirements for membership
_____e. Expectations of members after joining
_____f. Policies for disciplining/excluding members
_____g. Training for witnessing/evangelism
_____h. Training in spiritual disciplines (prayer, study, etc.)
_____i. Plan of salvation
_____j. Examination of the church covenant
_____k. Inventory of spiritual gifts
_____l. Explanation of the church's mission and/or vision
_____m. Structure, history, polity, etc., of the denomination
_____n. Introductions to church staff and leadership
_____o. Current opportunities for service in the church
_____p. Tithing/financial support of the church
_____q. Examination of the church constitution
_____r. Structure/support of missions through the Cooperative Program
_____s. Method/meaning of baptism
_____t. Purpose of the Lord's Supper
_____u. Tour of the church facilities
_____v. Other: _____

65. If your church uses a specific book, study guide, or kit for the new member/orientation class, what resource do you use?

66. Assume that a *new convert* has made a profession of faith in your church. For each of the following follow-up activities with that convert, please mark *when* that activity takes place. If your church does not use the follow-up activity, please mark N/A.

	Activity	N/A	Within 24 hrs.	Within 48 hrs.	Within 1 Week	Within 1 Month
a.	Counseled by a decision counselor					
b.	Provided a Bible					
c.	Given information explaining baptism					
d.	Assigned to a deacon or shepherd group					
e.	Contacted by a deacon or shepherd group leader					
f.	Assigned to a Bible study group or Sunday School class					
g.	Contacted by a Bible study group or Sunday School class leader					
h.	Assigned to a sponsor/discipler					
i.	Contacted by a sponsor/discipler					
j.	Contacted via a letter/phone call from church staff					
k.	Contacted via a visit from church staff					
l.	Provided offering envelopes					
m.	Baptized into church membership					
n.	Given a church directory					
o.	Provided a tour of church facility					
p.	Given study material for new believers					
q.	Other: _____					

67. New converts often find Christ through a number of different opportunities. Please estimate the percentage of baptized converts in your church *in the last year* whose *primary influence* in coming to Christ was each of the following:

67a. A friend/family member/coworker introduced them to Christ and invited them to church. _____%

67b. They attended church on their own and met Christ during a regular worship service. _____%

67c. A church member invited them to a special event or a revival service, where they accepted Christ. _____%

67d. They enrolled in a Bible study class and found Christ through Bible study and Christian fellowship. _____%

67e. They accepted Christ through a door-to-door witnessing or survey program. _____%

67f. A radio or television ministry introduced them to Christ. _____%

67g. Someone previously unknown to them unexpectedly shared the message of Christ with them. _____%

67h. Other: _____%

68. What positions/opportunities for service in the church does your church allow new converts to assume, i.e., what positions are open to new converts?

69. What method does your church use to introduce new converts to the congregation?

70. Please describe the church's process, if any, for connecting new members with other members in the church body, i.e., how does the church help new members develop relationships in the church?

71. Does the church periodically review membership records?   Yes ___   No ____
                                                              How often? _____

72. If the church reviews membership records, what parameters are used for determining a member's active/inactive status?   N/A ____

73. What is your church's practice toward reclaiming inactive members?

____a. Because our membership covenant requires attendance, we remove the member from our roll; we do not, however, discontinue outreach/ministry toward that person.

____ b. We place inactive members on an inactive list, but we do not have a specific plan in place to reclaim them.

____ c. Inactive members are placed on an inactive list; we try to reclaim them by the following plan: _____

____ d. Our church does not place members on an inactive list, nor do we have a plan for reclaiming inactive members.

____e. Other: _____

VII. TRAINING/SMALL GROUPS

74. Which of the following best describes the church's programs for developing believers?

____a. Traditional age-group Discipleship Training program studies prior to the P.M. service ____b. Traditional age-group Discipleship Training program studies, but scheduled at a time other than Sunday evening

____c. Varied short-term studies held prior to the P.M. service

____d. Varied short-term studies held at various times throughout the year

____e. One-to-one discipleship mentoring: a leader invites one person to study and work with him/her until growth is achieved and ministry is reproduced

____f. Group discipleship mentoring: a leader invites others to study and work with him/her until growth is achieved and ministry is reproduced

____g. Other: _____

75. At this point in your church's life, what is your evaluation of the overall effectiveness of the church's Discipleship Training program?

_____ a. Nonexistent

_____ b. Very poor/not effective at all

_____ c. Poor/only slightly effective

_____ d. Fair/somewhat effective

_____ e. Good/effective

_____ f. Excellent/very effective

76. If your church has a system for helping members discover their spiritual gifts and a place of service, please describe that system:

____a. Our church does not presently have a system for the spiritual gifts discovery and utilization.

____b. Our church does have a system that includes the following:

Spiritual gifts inventory used: _____

When the inventory is administered:_____

Process for keeping a record of members' gifts: _____

Process for coordinating members' gifts and church needs: _____

77. If your church offers a one-to-one mentoring/discipleship program, please describe that program:

____a. Our church does not presently have any program of a one-to-one mentoring/ discipleship.

____b. Our church does have a program that includes the following:

Material/literature used:_____

Number of sessions and time per session required: _____

Course *required* for:

_____ *all* new members

_____ *all* new converts

_____ not required, but offered

78. For each of the following types of small group and/or age-group studies, estimate the percentage of the resident membership that have participated in that type of study *in the last year*. Then, using the scale below, state the importance of that study to the church's overall assimilation process. If your church does not offer a particular group or study, please mark the N/A column.

1	2	3	4	5
Not Important at All	Only Slightly Important	Important	Very Important but Not Essential	Essential

	Type of Study	N/A	% Involved	Importance
78a.	Equipping centers			
78b.	*Evangelism Explosion*			
78c.	*Continuous Witness Training*			
78d.	*Survival Kit*			
78e.	*Experiencing God*			
78f.	Baptist doctrine studies			
78g.	Annual missions studies			
78h.	Church Study Course opportunities			
78i.	*PrayerLife*			
78j.	*MasterLife*			
78k.	*Precept* Bible studies			
78l.	Life Support studies (*Codependency, Steps to Significance*, etc.)			
78m.	Support groups			
78n.	Stewardship training or emphases			
78o.	Other: _____			

79. Please estimate the *number* of small groups offered through your church (including all Sunday School classes, discipleship classes, etc.).

80. What percentage of the small groups available in your church have been started within the past two years? _____%

81. What programs or methods does the church use to train the members in stewardship?

VIII. PASTORAL CARE

82. If your church has a plan by which it has a personal touch with *every* resident member at least once a year, please describe that plan.

    _____a. Our church does not have such a plan.

    _____b. Our church has a plan that operates as follows:

83. If your church has developed a *specific* process to attempt to assure that no members requiring pastoral care (members in the hospital, deaths in the family, job loss, etc.) are overlooked, please describe that plan:

    ____a. Our church does not have such a plan.
    ____b. Our church has a plan that operates as follows: _____

84. Who is most responsible for implementing, coordinating, and evaluating this process of pastoral care follow-up?
    ____a. Pastor
    ____b. Staff member (title)
    ____c. Layperson (position)
    ____d. Sunday School care group leaders
    ____e. Deacons, through a family ministry or shepherding plan
    ____f. Cell group leaders
    ____g. Other: _____

85. How much time typically lapses between a member's absence on Sunday and a contact from someone in the church?
    ____a. Less than one day
    ____b. One to seven days
    ____c. One to two weeks
    ____d. Two to four weeks
    ____e. The time varies because there is no established plan for follow-up.

86. Please rank the three most frequently cited reasons that members leave your church, with one (1) being the most common.
    ____a. Transfer of job to another location
    ____b. Interpersonal conflict in the church
    ____c. Disagreement with church doctrine
    ____d. Disagreement with the church's vision or plans
    ____e. Participation in a new church start or mission
    ____f. Unfriendliness of the church
    ____g. Boring or irrelevant sermons and programs
    ____h. Wounded feelings
    ____i. Apathy toward church in general
    ____j. Anger toward God
    ____k. A feeling of being "not needed" in the church
    ____l. Other: _____

IX. MISSIONS

87. What percentage of undesignated receipts does your church send to the Southern Baptist Convention's Cooperative Program? _____%

88. What percentage of your church's overall budget is committed to missions (including the Cooperative Program, associational missions, local missions, and other mission expenditures)? _____%

89. How many new church starts or missions has your church sponsored or cosponsored in the last three years?

90. What percentage of your resident membership has participated in mission activities (mission trips, mission starts, etc.) in the last year? _____%

91. Please list any social ministries (homeless shelters, food banks, pregnancy crisis centers, etc.) your church supports through personnel or funding.

X. OTHER INFORMATION

92. How much does your church utilize a computer to facilitate your assimilation process?

_____a. Not at all

_____b. Very little

_____c. Occasionally

_____d. Frequently

93. If your church uses a computer to facilitate your assimilation process, what computer program are you using? _____

94. If you could change without opposition *one* component of your church's overall assimilation process, what would that change be? _____

95. Does your church budget include a specific item for assimilation of guests and new members (although it may not be listed under that specific term)?

_____ a. Our church has no specific budget item for assimilation.

_____ b. We have a specific budget item for assimilation listed as : _____

96. Approximately what percentage of your church's budget is devoted to programs/personnel/ministries that primarily relate to assimilation (whether or not *assimilation* is specifically listed)?   _____%

97. What events/activities does the church use to recognize or honor laypersons who serve faithfully in church positions?

98. What other question(s) about assimilation should we have asked? Please feel free to propose an answer to any question you include.

99. Now that you have completed this survey, what findings have surprised you about your church's assimilation process?

100. To help us complete this survey, please provide the names and phone numbers of *five* church members who have joined your church in the past year who would be willing to conduct a phone interview with Graham School personnel. If possible, please include the name of at least three *recent converts*. Please be aware that we may not call all the names submitted.

Name	Phone
1. _____	_____
2. _____	_____
3. _____	_____
4. _____	_____
5. _____	_____

If your church requires a signed membership covenant, we would also like to receive a copy of the covenant. Please return the survey and any other enclosures in the included envelope.

We at the Billy Graham School of Missions, Evangelism, and Church Growth at The Southern Baptist Theological Seminary thank you for participating in this extensive but important survey. Our prayer is that God will use this information to further His work in growing Great Commission churches.

Notes

Introduction

1. Thom S. Rainer, *Effective Evangelistic Churches* (Nashville: Broadman & Holman, 1996).

Chapter 1

1. Thom S. Rainer, *Giant Awakenings* (Nashville: Broadman & Holman, 1995), see especially 113–18.

2. For more information on this generation, see Thom S. Rainer, *The Bridger Generation* (Nashville: Broadman & Holman, 1997). Several parts of the book deal with the issue of the church reaching and retaining this second largest generation in America's history.

3. See Thom S. Rainer, *Effective Evangelistic Churches* (Nashville: Broadman & Holman, 1996).

Chapter 2

1. The results of this study are published in Thom S. Rainer, *Giant Awakenings* (Nashville: Broadman & Holman, 1995).

2. This study was published as Thom S. Rainer, *Effective Evangelistic Churches* (Nashville: Broadman & Holman, 1996).

3. George Barna, *Virtual America: What Every Church Leader Needs to Know about Ministry in an Age of Spiritual and Technological Revolution* (Ventura, Calif.: Regal, 1993), 52–55.

4. This study was published in *Vanishing Boundaries* (Louisville: Westminster/John Knox, 1995).

5. See Rainer, *Effective Evangelistic Churches,* particularly chapter 5.

6. Robert Wuthnow, "How Small Groups Are Transforming Our Lives," *Christianity Today* (7 February 1994), 23.

7. Ibid.

Chapter 3

1. An entire book will eventually be written by Chuck Lawless on this aspect of the study. The book is tentatively titled *Entry Points* and should be available in 2000.

Chapter 4

1. Thom S. Rainer, *Effective Evangelistic Churches* (Nashville: Broadman & Holman, 1996).

Chapter 5

1. See Thom S. Rainer, *Effective Evangelistic Churches* (Nashville: Broadman & Holman, 1996).

Chapter 6

1. The calculation of the retention ratio in a given year was as follows: (Worship attendance in year X minus worship attendance in year X-1) divided by (total number of new members added in year X).

2. The best writing on this topic is Don R. Cox, "The Shifting Role of Formative Church Discipline in the Evangelistic Strategy of Southern Baptist Convention Churches 1955–1995." Unpublished Ph.D. dissertation, Southern Baptist Theological Seminary, 1998.

3. See Thom S. Rainer, *Effective Evangelistic Churches* (Nasvhille: Broadman & Holman, 1996), chapter 9.

Chapter 8

1. The study is reported in Thom S. Rainer, *Effective Evangelistic Churches* (Nashville: Broadman & Holman, 1996).

Chapter 9

1. A good work on this perspective is William D. Hendricks, *Exit Interviews* (Chicago: Moody, 1993).

2. See Thom S. Rainer, *Effective Evangelistic Churches* (Nashville: Broadman & Holman, 1996), especially chapter 10.

Chapter 10

1. The fascinating story of Saddleback Valley Community Church is told in Rick Warren's *The Purpose Driven Church* (Grand Rapids: Zondervan, 1995). See especially chapter 1.

2. For more about "eating an elephant," see Thom S. Rainer, *Eating the Elephant* (Nashville: Broadman & Holman, 1994).

3. See Thom S. Rainer, *Effective Evangelistic Churches* (Nashville: Broadman & Holman, 1996), especially pages 4, 21 22, 28, 41, 64, 96.

Index